PRODUCTIVE
PERFORMANCE
APPRAISALS

The WorkSmart Series

PRODUCTIVE
PERFORMANCE
APPRAISALS

Randi Toler Sachs

amacom

AMERICAN MANAGEMENT ASSOCIATION
THE WORKSMART SERIES

New York • Atlanta • Boston • Chicago • Kansas City • San Francisco • Washington, D.C.
Brussels • Toronto • Mexico City

This book is available at a special
discount when ordered in bulk quantities.
For information, contact Special Sales Department,
AMACOM, a division of American Management Association,
135 West 50th Street, New York, NY 10020.

This publication is designed to provide accurate and authoritative information in regard to the subject matter covered. It is sold with the understanding that the publisher is not engaged in rendering legal, accounting, or other professional service. If legal advice or other expert assistance is required, the services of a competent professional person should be sought.

Library of Congress Cataloging-in-Publication Data

Sachs, Randi Toler.
    Productive performance appraisals/Randi Toler Sachs.
       p.   cm.—(The WorkSmart series)
    ISBN 0-8144-7796-8
    1. Employees—Rating of. I. Title. II. Series.
HF5549.5.R3S22 1992
  658.3'125—dc20   92-20830
                                CIP

Printing number

10 9 8 7 6 5 4 3 2 1

CONTENTS

PART III. COMMON PROBLEMS AND EFFECTIVE SOLUTIONS

PART IV. WRAPPING IT UP

PREFACE

Does the thought of conducting performance appraisals for your employees make you cringe? Is it something you tend to put off until you "have the time"? Does the idea of telling grown men or women that they have not been "living up to their potential" make your palms sweat and your throat dry? Don't feel bad. You are not alone.

Many supervisors look upon performance appraisals as one of the most uncomfortable tasks that they are called upon to do, and had they a say in it they might eliminate altogether any formal meeting that could be called a performance appraisal. But their feelings—and yours—are a waste of energy. Performance appraisals serve a very useful role in the workplace. And believe it or not, they need not be unpleasant for you.

It is not unusual for those who rise from the ranks or come from initial management training to find it uncomfortable to "get personal" and evaluate another person's performance—especially face to face! You probably have a number of reasons why the review of one employee or another will give you trouble. The employee may be a discipline problem; she may be very sensitive; he may have nowhere to go within your organization . . . The possibilities are as numerous as there are employees.

This book will help you overcome your fear of conducting performance appraisals by giving you straightforward advice on:

- How to prepare for each employee's interview
- How to structure a performance appraisal
- How to put yourself and your employees at ease

- How to make your performance appraisal collaborative efforts between yourself and your employees
- How to strengthen your relationship with your employee by conducting a productive review
- How to handle problem employees

Most important, this book will help you develop your own style for giving performance appraisals. By following the advice presented here, you can make your performance appraisals the useful, productive, and very necessary management tools that they can be.

PART I

THE PRODUCTIVE APPRAISAL

CHAPTER 1

WHAT'S THE POINT?

"You wanted to see me, Ed?"

"Yes, Dan, come right in. As you know, it's been six months since your last performance appraisal. I want you to know that I've been very pleased with your work. I feel I can really count on you when I need something done right."

"Thanks, Ed. That's nice to hear."

"Tell me, how has everything been going on your end? Is there anything you would like to talk about? I've got some time now, for a change."

"Gee, I can't think of anything right now. Except that . . ."

"What is it, Dan?"

"Well, ever since they moved the coffee machine near my work-station, I've been bothered by all the noise and conversation that seem to go along with the coffee."

"We'll just move it then. I don't want one of my top workers distracted like that. Just give me a few days, okay?"

"Sure, Ed. Thanks."

"As you know, management has had to limit merit increases to once a year now. Since you received a raise six months ago, you'll have to wait another six months before we can do anything about your salary. But if you keep up the good work, there should be nothing to worry about."

"Okay, Ed. Thanks for the good words."

"You're very welcome. And thank you. You make my job that much easier."

Ed, the supervisor in the preceding scenario, is probably feeling very happy with himself. He can check that performance appraisal off his "to do" list now. He believes that he has fulfilled his obligations by telling his employee that he has been doing a great job and to "keep up the good work."

"These types of performance appraisals are simple," Ed says to himself. "I have no complaints, and money is not an issue. These types of appraisals are short and sweet. Now I can get back to work."

Poor Ed is under an all-too-common delusion that performance appraisals are used either to give a good employee a pat on the back or to put the pressure on an unsatisfactory employee to improve his or her performance. What Ed doesn't know is that performance appraisals require advance preparation and that the meeting itself can and should be a collaborative planning session during which both supervisor and employee can take an in-depth look at past and current performances and can together make plans for the future.

Whether your employee is a good worker or a thorn in your side, you can make your performance appraisals productive sessions that will benefit you both.

By reading this book you've taken the first step in deciding to make the performance appraisals you give truly worthwhile. For many of us, reviewing the work of others is one of the more difficult aspects of being a supervisor. You may not feel fully qualified to play judge and jury over the quality of each employee's work. However, if you follow the advice offered here, you can actually eliminate some of the burden of that responsibility. By making the performance appraisal a collaborative effort, you will ultimately share some of the decision making with your employee. More important, you will be able to use your performance appraisals to improve the productivity of your employees and, ultimately, of your entire department.

A produc-
tive ap-
praisal rec-
ognizes
that people
are the
valuable
resource of
any organi-
zation.

HOW CAN APPRAISALS BE PRODUCTIVE?

A common misconception is that the sole purpose of an appraisal is to inform an employee how his or her performance has been rated. Unfortunately, this is often all that is done. A productive performance appraisal, however, can accomplish much more (see Figure 1-1). A productive appraisal, along with providing a review of the employee's work, serves as a work session between supervisor and employee in which you take the time and effort to meet with an individual employee and set new goals and objectives for the coming year. A productive appraisal recognizes that *people* are the most valuable resource of any organization.

In reviewing the above discussion between Ed and Dan, what do you notice about employee Dan's part in the conversa-

Figure 1-1.   Benefits of productive performance appraisals.

- Employee learns of his or her own strengths in addition to weaknesses.
- New goals and objectives are agreed upon.
- Employee is an active participant in the evaluation process.
- The relationship between supervisor and employees is taken to an adult-to-adult level.
- Work teams may be restructured for maximum efficiency.
- Employee renews his or her interest in being a part of the organization now and in the future.
- Training needs are identified.
- Time is devoted to discussing quality of work without regard to money issues.
- Supervisor becomes more comfortable in reviewing the performance of employees.
- Employees feel that they are taken seriously as individuals and that the supervisor is truly concerned about their needs and goals.

tion? If you said, "There wasn't much to it," you're on the right track. Ed really didn't give Dan much of an opportunity to talk. In fact, most of his questions required little more than one-word answers.

One reason you may dread giving performance reviews is that you feel obligated to do most of the talking—that you must have a prepared speech to give your employee. However, in a productive appraisal this is not the case. Your appraisal session should not be a one-way monologue. Instead, you should meet with your employee and engage in a true conversation. In addition to giving your own opinions about the employee's past performance and future potential, you should listen carefully to what he or she has to say. Furthermore, you will actually make decisions about future assignments and goals based on what both you and the employee decide *together*.

In Ed's "review" of Dan, not a word was said about preparing new goals for the coming year. Ed's reasoning may have been that because he was not promoting Dan and there were no problems with performance or productivity, a new goal-setting session would not be necessary. Ed is wrong, of course. Even the best performers should be given new goals to strive for, or their interest in the job may wane. It's natural for people to want to better themselves, to earn the intrinsic rewards of doing well and improving. Even if job titles or responsibilities do not change appreciably, goals can be set to improve efficiency and quality of work and new objectives can be identified. Indeed, by neglecting to set new goals, you may be giving the message that if the employee wants to move ahead, he or she will have to do it at another place of work.

IT'S THE PROCESS THAT COUNTS

Okay, you say. I agree that it is important to set new goals for each of my employees periodically, and performance reviews are certainly convenient times to do this. But isn't the supervisor the best judge of what these goals should be? After all, I know the direction that the entire department will be headed in the coming year. I know where I can best use each of my employees. Wouldn't it be better to present each employee with my own findings and see if we are in agreement?

Our short answer to the above statements is a succinct no. Here are a few reasons why:

- When goals are set without input from the employee, there is much less motivation for these goals to be realized.
- The direction of the department must reflect the interests, abilities, and motivations of the employees who comprise it or it will be a continual, up-hill battle for the supervisor to meet these objectives.
- Presented wtih a set of objectives predetermined by the supervisor, most employees will accept them not only as what they need to do to meet with full approval from their supervisor, but they will also believe that their abilities are limited to the list of goals they are given.

The most important benefit, however, can be described as the secret weapon—what makes it all worthwhile. That is that the most important result of the performance appraisal is not that the employee is given a rating of the quality of his or her work; it is not that the employee comes away from the meeting with new performance objectives and career goals; and it is not that the employee has been given enough positive feedback to last him or her for another six months or a year (which, by the way, is never the case).

The most important result of the performance appraisal is the actual process itself.

The most important result of the performance appraisal is the actual process itself. By working together to analyze and evaluate the employee's performance, his or her place within the department and the organization as a whole, and by setting goals for the near and long-term future, you and your employee can strengthen your relationship and become a team of two adults working toward a common, agreed-upon goal.

In the following chapters you will learn how to change the performance appraisals you give your employees from semi-annual pep talks to work sessions that will help the employee continue to grow in his or her job and will help you renew that employee's commitment to the organization.

Whether you are a novice supervisor or an old hand, you can improve the quality of the reviews you give. We realize, of course, that many companies have set policies and guidelines that require you to carry out performance appraisals in a certain way. However, the message in this book can transcend different vehicles for its use. Take what you can from us and adapt it for your own personal use. For a sample of what is to come, take the Do You or Don't You? test that follows to see how many of our techniques you are already using. When you are done, continue reading. You'll find that conducting productive appraisals is not as hard as you may think.

TEST YOURSELF:
DO YOU OR DON'T YOU?

To how many of the following statements regarding performance appraisals and your feelings about them can you say "I Do"?

	I Do	I Don't
I keep a performance log on each of my employees and update it frequently.	————	————
I prepare my employees in advance of reviews and ask them to complete a self-evaluation sheet.	————	————
I treat monetary issues and promotions separate from performance appraisal discussions.	————	————
I get my employee's input before making decisions on reassignments or new tasks.	————	————
I hold all performance reviews in a private setting at a time when we will not be disturbed.	————	————
I know how to give an employee criticism without arousing hostility.	————	————
I know what "not to say" in a performance review.	————	————
I feel giving performance reviews is a good use of my time.	————	————
I feel comfortable giving performance appraisals to all of my employees.	————	————
I always follow up on areas of concern that come up during appraisal interviews.	————	————
I discuss both what the employee has done right and wrong during a performance review.	————	————

CHAPTER 2

IT'S EASY AS ONE, TWO, THREE

Employees should be as prepared for appraisals as you are.

If you want to get the maximum value out of the performance appraisals you give, you have to put some effort into the process. An ideal performance appraisal is actually a three-step affair. Let's go over each individual step first, and then discuss why all three are needed to do the job right.

STEP 1: EVALUATION AND JOB ANALYSIS

An employee who is scheduled for a performance appraisal deserves to be as prepared as you are. The appraisal interview is the employee's time to discuss any problems he or she is having on the job and also to ask your advice on career development. Asking an employee into your office at the last minute to meet for a performance appraisal is not only unfair but gives the impression that you are trying to avoid something.

The best way to prepare yourself and your employee for the meeting is for each of you to fill out complementary forms (see Figures 3-1 and 3-2 in Chapter 3) that cover two major areas:

1. *Job Analysis*, which is an evaluation and analysis of what the job itself entails. It identifies and assigns weight to each of the employee's areas of accountability.
2. *Performance/Work Habits Review*, which assigns a numerical rating for each characteristic.

10

It can be quite a revelation just how differently you and your employees perceive their jobs.

You can create your own forms to best suit your needs. Figures 3-1 and 3-2 in Chapter 3 should give you a good starting point. Give your employee these forms three to five working days (weekends do not count) before the appraisal meeting and ask him or her to come to the meeting prepared to discuss the following:

- Job performance since the last review
- Personal career objectives
- Problems or concerns about the present job
- Things the employee would like to see change for him- or herself personally and for the department in general
- Goals for improving future performance and productivity

On the Job Analysis form (Figure 3-1), the employee is asked to list all major job responsibilities and to give them a "weight," the percentage of time on the job that the employee spends on each of those tasks. At the same time, you should fill out an identical form for the employee, giving your own perception of what the job entails. The first time you try this, it can be quite a revelation just how differently you and your employees perceive their jobs. Let's listen in on what one supervisor learns when she tries this method for the first time.

Dorothy: Stanley, did you really mean to say that 50 percent of your time at work is spent helping your co-workers with their problems and questions?

Stanley: Yes, I did. I don't have to tell you that I've been with this department longer than anybody. People are always coming to me with questions and I never turn them away. Sometimes, it does get hard to do my own work on time, but I manage, don't I?

Dorothy: Yes, you do. I wonder, though, if this is really the best use of your time. Let me ask you something: Do you find yourself answering the same types of questions over and over, or is it constantly new problems?

Stanley: Actually, it's a lot of the same thing. Not to complain, but I find that some of the newer employees do use me as a crutch at times. They realize it's easier and faster to ask me how to do something than to figure it out on their own. Really, I don't mind.

Dorothy is upset with herself for letting this go on without her knowledge, but she doesn't let it get the best of her. After she has some time to think about the situation, she comes up with an idea for utilizing Stanley's knowledge and improving productivity for all the department members involved.

Dorothy: Stanley, how would you feel about working with me to develop a training program—it might just take a few sessions—to get these people to start thinking for themselves? Not only would the rest of the department benefit, but it would be good managerial experience for you. I'd like you to help me lead the sessions as well as choose what to include.

Stanley: It sounds like an interesting project, Dorothy. I'd be willing to give it a try. I also think that we could work up a type of resource manual that we can distribute to everyone in the department. What do you think?

Dorothy: I think it's a great idea. Thanks, Stanley. I'm feeling very optimistic about this venture.

The Job Analysis form you give the employee is basically a blank sheet of paper with space for listing job responsibilities and tasks, the objectives of those tasks, and the percentage of the job it requires. The Performance/Work Habits Review form (Figure 3-2) should list those qualities that you believe pertain to that employee and his or her job. Both you and the employee independently rate the employee on a scale of one to five for each trait. You may find the same form applicable for all of your employees, or you may adapt it to the individual being interviewed. Remember, make sure to give the employee ample time to complete the forms and to

A working session can change employee expectations about the performance appraisal.

think over what he or she would like to discuss at the appraisal interview. Then you are ready for Step 2.

STEP 2: THE APPRAISAL INTERVIEW

Until now, you may have always begun your performance appraisal process by jumping right into Step 2. Let's discuss the differences between that kind of appraisal and a truly productive performance appraisal. In Chapter 6, we talk about specific methods for conducting the interview that will help make you more comfortable in your role of performance reviewer.

Many supervisors start an appraisal interview by saying something positive about the employee. What's wrong with that? Nothing at all. But we want to get beyond superficial compliments and discuss specific performance traits that we admire in the employee as well as those that need improvement.

Traditionally, employees view a performance appraisal as an ordeal they must go through before they can find out whether or not they will receive a salary increase, just how much that increase will be, and when and if they can ever expect to receive a promotion. By asking your employee to join you in a working session, you can change the expectations that your employees now have when they think about participating in a performance appraisal.

If this is new to your employees, it may take some time to get them to let their guards down and cooperate fully. But if you take the right approach, you should not encounter too much trouble. Think of it like this: You are asking employees to talk about their favorite topic—themselves.

Explain from the onset that you will not be discussing money issues at this meeting. Assure the employee that you will set up a separate meeting to talk that over in the near future. That may take some time to sink in, but when it does, it frees you to talk solely about job performance and setting objectives for the future.

Because you have prepared your employee for the appraisal interview, there will be plenty to discuss. By filling out the forms in Figures 3-1 and 3-2, you have each provided yourselves with written evaluations that you can compare and discuss. In addition, the employee has been forced to think about what he or she is doing in the job and how that does or does not help meet ultimate career aspirations. Now, instead of spending the time you have with your employee justifying and explaining exactly how you came up with the amount of money in the proposed salary increase, you can talk about the quality of the employee's performance without worrying that your observations don't match up with a "high," "medium," or "low" increase. You have set the scene well for a genuinely productive meeting.

STEP 3: THE POSTAPPRAISAL MEETING

Eventually, you will have to discuss salary issues with each of your employees. Although such a meeting should be separate (at least two or three days later) from the appraisal interview, the final outcome should reflect what was decided upon during that interview. For example, an interview in which it was determined that the employee is ready for promotion should ideally be followed with either a promotion or a pledge that promotion will come as soon as it is permissible within company guidelines.

You must be careful not to promise anything that you will not be able to deliver. If you believe that the money you have to offer an employee will be a disappointment, be prepared to explain the company guidelines you followed.

Although salary may be the most important issue of the meeting in the employee's view, you should also take the opportunity to review the objectives you have set for the coming year and to sum up the general performance rating you have given the employee. You may also have some new responsibilities or assignments to give the employee at this meeting. Be sure to point out the connection between what was discussed at the appraisal interview and the new assignments. Let the employee know that you are available for assistance in learning any new responsibilities he or she will be taking on and that you will be meeting with the employee in the near future to discuss his or her progress in reaching newly determined goals.

CHAPTER 3

FACE TO FACE

Now that we have identified why you may want to change your method of preparing for and conducting employee performance appraisals, let's look at how best to handle such an interview when you finally come face to face.

A GOOD BEGINNING

Because most employees are nervous about what will be said at their performance reviews, you can help make the meeting more pleasant by trying to put the employee at ease right away.

Harvey: Come in and sit down, Matthew. Please don't look so nervous. We both know you're a good programmer and there are no major problems to bog us down, don't we?

Matthew: I guess so.

Harvey: Then, please try to relax. The purpose of this meeting is so that we can evaluate your performance together and also so that we can work together to plan the best path for your future. Have you brought the forms I asked you to fill out?

Matthew: Yes. I have them right here.

Harvey: Excellent. I've filled out the same forms. I want to compare what we've each written on the Job Analysis form so we can see just how well we agree on what are your major job responsibilities.

Harvey is doing a fine job of beginning the interview. Right away, he has let Matthew know that the performance appraisal is going to be a positive one. Also, by acknowledging that there is natural tension, he has helped to dissipate some of that, too. By not attempting to cover up the purpose of the meeting with a lot of small talk, Harvey sets the tone for getting right down to the business at hand, once he has promised Matthew that there is nothing to fear.

Using the Job Analysis form (Figure 3-1) to begin the meeting is a good idea, too. Harvey and Matthew can talk about the objectives of the job before they get into a discussion on just how well Matthew is doing. When Harvey and Matthew come to an area in which they have given different weights, Harvey discusses it calmly and with an open mind, but he sticks to his agenda.

Harvey: I see that you've given New Programming a weight of 15 percent and Project Support a weight of 25 percent. I've got the weights of those two switched here, with 25 percent for New Programming and 15 percent for Project Support.

Matthew: Really? I wouldn't mind if that were the case, because, frankly, I enjoy writing new programs. But it seems to me that I definitely spend more time on project support.

Harvey: If that's the case, that's going to change. I really need your talents used to develop new programs. In fact, I'd like to see the weight changed next time we meet to closer to 35 percent of your time spent on new and updated programs. Tell me, why do you think you spend so much time on support?

Matthew: I think it's because the users are always coming to me with bits and pieces of things they want to do or want to change. Maybe if there were better communica-

Figure 3-1. Job Analysis.*

Employee: Matthew Gaber

Job Title: Programmer/Systems Analyst

Department: Data Processing Systems and Programming

Responsibilities of Job	Functional Objectives	Weight
New programming	Create programs to increase DPS efficiency	25%
Project support	Update existing systems and programs	15%
User assistance	Explain systems functions to users; adapt programs for user needs	20%
Technical knowledge	Maintain current technical skills; master new hardware	15%
Problem solving	Offer quick response to problems; maintain calm and professional attitude	15%
Communications	Send and receive information effectively and in a timely manner	10%

*Note that this form is written for a very specific position, whereas the form in Figure 3-2 can be used for just about any type of employee.

tion we could accomplish more at one time, and then the job of ongoing support would take less time and energy.

Harvey: That's a good thought. I agree with you, and I've got some ideas about improving those communications. I'll also be talking to the supervisor of the user department that you work with and see if maybe we can work something out together.

Matthew: That would be great.

DISCUSSING QUALITY OF PERFORMANCE

Once you and the employee have come to an agreement on just what the job entails and what he or she should be doing, you can then move onto the issue of quality of performance. This is where you can easily get into trouble. Unless you are careful about what you say to your employee you can end up: (1) causing resentment between the employee and yourself, (2) getting the wrong message across to the employee, or (3) saying nothing of major significance and wasting the opportunity to help the employee improve performance.

Harvey, for the most part, is pleased with Matthew's performance. He does have some suggestions for improvement, however.

Harvey: I'd like you to know, Matthew, that I think you're a good employee and that you are an asset to the programming department. Your programming technique has improved over the past six months. I was especially pleased with the way you handled the accounting program.

Matthew: Thanks. I worked hard on that program and I was happy with the way it turned out.

Harvey: If I have to pick one area where I feel you need the most improvement, it would be in communications. As you said before, you notice that communications between programming and users is not always the most efficient. I think part of it is that you still lack the experience to get to the bottom of what your users need. I think that by consulting with them a little more closely and by asking more questions before you start a project, you may find that the results will be more satisfying.

Matthew: I never thought of that before.

Harvey: You know, there is someone whom you could learn a lot from in this regard. She really has a knack for dealing with users. I'm talking about Joan Houlihan. How do you feel about working with her for a while?

Matthew: What do you mean?

Harvey: I'm about to ask Joan to head a new project group for the manufacturing research department. I'd like you to work on that team and also to observe how Joan works with the users to get the project underway. I can ask her to utilize you as associate group leader. In this way you can be in on the interdepartmental negotiations and you can also get some more experience in project planning.

Matthew: That sounds very interesting.

Harvey: You understand that Joan would be in charge of leading the group project, but that you would be her chief assistant. This is for her benefit, too, of course. I think your technical skills are the best of the group for this application, and I think you can help guide the other programmers on the team.

Matthew: Terrific. That answers my question about how I can get more leadership experience.

Harvey: I knew you would ask me about that, Matthew, and you have every right to. I do believe you have leadership potential, but I want to make sure you can handle all aspects of project management when I ask you to take on your own team.

Harvey really has come prepared to this appraisal meeting. He has identified Matthew's weak point (user communications) and also has anticipated that Matthew would be eager to strive toward heading a project (a career objective that had been established in the previous appraisal). Harvey has already decided on a way to help both needs, and he presents it to Matthew in such a positive light that Matthew is, of course, pleased with being given the opportunity to achieve while learning at the same time.

Once you have given your overall impression of the employee's performance, discussing specific areas and incidents that concern you, you can turn to the Performance/Work Habits Review form (Figure 3-2) and compare what each of you perceive to be the employee's strong and weak points. This form can conveniently serve to summarize and pinpoint some of the things you may have just discussed. By identifying these traits on the form as "work habits," the employee can see how some of the specific behaviors you've discussed can translate into a general impression of his or her competence.

If your employee has been honest in his or her self-evaluation, there should not be a great deal of disparity between your form and the employee's. Typically, an employee will rate him- or herself with more "4s" and "5s" than does the supervisor, who sees the room for improvement that an employee still has. If you have 3s where an employee has rated 4s, it's not worth quibbling over. Point out that you agree the employee is doing well, and there is still room for improvement. Tell the employee what you like about what he or she is doing in this area. For example, "You consistently meet your deadlines. I appreciate that and hope that you can continue to be so reliable." Remember to point out the positive marks you have given the employee and try to cite specific examples that influenced your giving the high rating.

Concentrate on areas in which either of you has circled "1" or "2" when you talk about what areas need to be improved. For example, Matthew had been having difficulty getting to work on time, but he wasn't aware of how much of an impact it had made on his supervisor.

Harvey: I've only given you one rating of "1," Matthew, and that's in punctuality. I've spoken to you a number of times about getting into work late, but I still see you coming in late two or three times a week—that's a lot, Matthew.

Matthew: I know. But I always meet my deadlines, I always get my work done . . . I stay late if I have to. I just find it

Figure 3-2. Performance/Work Habits Review.*

Employee: Matthew Gaber

Job Title: Programmer/Systems Analyst

Department: Data Processing Systems and Programming

Check all items relevant to employee's position. Rate each item on a scale of one to five. Circle number at right.

> 1 = Needs much improvement
> 2 = Needs some improvement
> 3 = Satisfactory
> 4 = Very Good
> 5 = Excellent

Part I. General Work Habits and Attitude

a. Attendance/punctuality	1	2	3	4	5
b. Meets deadlines	1	2	3	4	5
c. Cooperates with coworkers	1	2	3	4	5
d. Accepts suggestions	1	2	3	4	5
e. Manages work schedule	1	2	3	4	5
f. Uses equipment properly	1	2	3	4	5
g. Prioritizes work well	1	2	3	4	5

Part II. Job Performance

a. Quality of work	1	2	3	4	5
b. Ability to solve problems	1	2	3	4	5
c. Uses original ideas	1	2	3	4	5
d. Communications abilities	1	2	3	4	5
e. Time management	1	2	3	4	5
f. Technical/professional knowledge	1	2	3	4	5
g. Hands-on skills	1	2	3	4	5
h. Interpersonal skills	1	2	3	4	5
i. Ability to work on a team	1	2	3	4	5

*Note that this form can be used for just about any type of employee, whereas the form in Figure 3-1 is written for a very specific position.

It's impor-
tant to
remember
that no-
body is per-
fect.

hard to get here by 9 o'clock. Is it really important what time I start, as long as I finish well?

Harvey: It *is* important, because you don't work in a vacuum, Matthew. Other people need to talk to you about your work and if you're not here when they are, you are causing them to waste their time. Is there a specific reason why you can't get here on time?

Matthew: No, but . . . What about Wendy? She comes in at 9:30 every day and leaves at 5:30.

Harvey: That's right. Wendy has to drop her child at a day care center that doesn't open until 8:45. That's the earliest she can get here, and so we've made that arrangement with her. Do you have a similar problem?

Matthew: No. I'm just not a naturally early riser.

Harvey: I wish we could accommodate everybody's inner clock, but we can't, Matthew. I have to tell you that you really need to discipline yourself to arrive at work on time. I'd hate for a relatively minor infraction to stand in the way of your advancement.

Matthew: I understand what you're saying. I'll be here on time from now on.

Harvey finally comes down hard on Matthew about his late arrivals. Although he pointed out the infractions when they happened, Harvey waits until the appraisal to really make an impression on Matthew. Here is where Harvey can be faulted. However, it is important to remember that nobody is perfect. If you realize that you've failed to change your employee's behavior through daily interaction, you can use the performance appraisal to finally get your point across. After all, there is something about seeing a shortcoming on paper that makes it impossible to ignore.

ASK FOR INPUT

A productive performance appraisal allows for give and take between you and your employee. Ask the employee how she

Avoid the cliches!

feels about the quality of her own performance and what she would like to change (see further discussion of this subject in Chapter 4). Harvey broaches the subject in this way:

Harvey: Matthew, have you given any thought to your strengths and weaknesses? What skills would you like to try to improve? What areas would you like to learn more about?

Matthew: Well, I'm pretty satisfied with my technical programming ability, but I would like to learn some additional languages. I would also like to improve my proficiency on other hardware and software systems.

Perhaps because Harvey has asked Matthew to come prepared to talk about this, he had an easy time in getting Matthew to identify what skills areas he would like to work on. When employees are not accustomed to thinking about their futures, it can be a lot more difficult to get the conversation going.

WATCH WHAT YOU SAY— AND HOW YOU SAY IT

Can you remember sitting at a performance review and hearing your supervisor say things that made you want to start whistling and looking at the ceiling? The feeling was probably very reminiscent of memories of lectures given to you by parents or teachers when your behavior came under scrutiny.

Too often, we revert to old, tried-and-true phrases to express ourselves. In other words, we use cliches. When we let this happen, we generally lose the attention of our audience and their belief that we are really attuned to them as individuals.

Listed below are some of the more common cliches—both negative and positive—embraced by supervisors at performance appraisal times. The first three examples show how you can express the same ideas in a more personal way by citing specific behavior. Then, you're on your own. Try to come up with more original ways to get your message across.

Cliche 1:
Amy, you're not living up to your potential.
More Personal:
I was sure that you had enough experience in this area to handle this assignment, Amy. Why do you think you've had trouble getting the work done correctly?

Cliche 2:
Richard, you make very good use of your time.
More Personal:
I'm pleased with the way I see you organize your workload, Richard. I was especially impressed with how you were able to finish that last assignment without having to work overtime.

Cliche 3:
Sharon, I feel sometimes your behavior is very immature.
More Personal:
The way you handled that complaint by Mr. Smith was inappropriate, Sharon. You have to control your temper and concentrate on solving the problem. Instead, you seemed to take his complaint personally, and you responded defensively instead of helpfully.

Now try some on your own:

- **Cliche 4:** You need to improve your productivity.

  _____

  _____

  _____

  _____

  _____

- **Cliche 5:** You get along well with others.

  _____
  _____
  _____
  _____
  _____

- **Cliche 6:** Your skills are not up to par.

  _____
  _____
  _____
  _____
  _____

- **Cliche 7:** You're not trying to do your best.

  _____
  _____
  _____
  _____
  _____

- **Cliche 8:** You're a pleasure to supervise.

  _____
  _____
  _____
  _____
  _____

- **Cliche 9:** You have to prove yourself before I can give you any more responsibility.

  _____
  _____
  _____
  _____
  _____

• **Cliche 10:** I wish I could do more to help you, but my hands are tied.

_____

_____

_____

_____

_____

SETTING THE SCENE

To give an appraisal interview your undivided attention and to make your employee as comfortable as possible, take the time to set the scene for a productive meeting. Use the following checklist to make sure you haven't forgotten anything.

CHECKLIST FOR SETTING THE SCENE

_____ Arrange to have all calls taken and visitors diverted.

_____ Make sure you have scheduled enough time for the meeting.

_____ Clear your desk of any extraneous papers or files that will get in the way of your working on the desk with forms and papers.

_____ Have temperature level in office comfortable—neither too cold nor too warm.

_____ Have a pitcher of water and cups handy, if possible.

_____ Put away anything you tend to fidget with, such as rubber bands, paper clips, etc.

_____ Have all necessary paperwork and forms ready.

_____ Provide employee with a comfortable chair.

PART

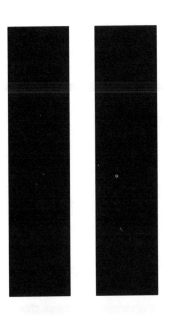

HOW TO MAKE IT HAPPEN: ADVANCE PREPARATIONS

CHAPTER 4

PLANNING FOR THE FUTURE

Almost every employee has hopes and aspirations beyond his present job.

Perhaps the most important part of any performance appraisal is the part that is quite often either left out completely or given very short shrift. But this is what can make the difference between a productive meeting and a superficial discussion. We are referring to, of course, the employee development and career objectives portion of the appraisal.

Almost every employee has hopes and aspirations beyond his or her present job. For some, these hopes remain distant wishes. But for those lucky enough to have the right supervisor and the necessary motivation, career objectives can become obtainable goals.

During each performance appraisal you should work with the employee to come up with a list of long-term and short-term career goals. Then, at the next appraisal meeting you should evaluate what progress has been made toward these goals, what new directions the employee's career has taken, and together you can decide if and how the employee's strategic plans should be changed.

HOW SUPERVISORS CAN HELP

Let's look at two examples of how supervisors help employees plan for their career futures. In the first example, Kathy, the employee, has definite ideas about what she would like to do in the future, but she needs help in planning how to attain her goal.

Sara: Let's talk about where you see yourself headed over the next few years, Kathy. You started two years ago as a public relations assistant and now you've moved up to an associate position. You've done very well in reaching the goals that you set for yourself a year ago. What's next? Can we make some plans for the future?

Kathy: Actually, I've been giving this a lot of thought—especially since you asked me to work on it last week. I enjoy writing press releases and articles for clients, but what I find most exciting is working on special events. I guess I like the variety of that and also the satisfaction of seeing the culmination of all my efforts come together rather spectacularly. I'd really like to make that my specialty, perhaps becoming a Special Events Coordinator for the department, but I don't know if that is possible. What do you think?

Sara: Well, I think that's an interesting idea. We haven't handled these types of assignments that way before, but that doesn't mean we can't explore the possibilities.

At this point, Sara is wise to be cautious about what she says to Kathy. Because Kathy is expressing interest in a different type of position from what currently exists within the department, it means they will have to devise a new type of career path for her to follow. It also means that eventually it would require the approval of upper management, and Sara would like to discuss it with her own boss to see whether the idea is plausible to him.

Sara: Let's think about what types of skills a Special Events Coordinator would need. Then we can devise a plan for how you can improve these skills, along with the ones we've already identified that you use in your present job. And I'm sure we'll find a great deal of overlap, anyway.

Kathy: That sounds like a good idea.

Together, Sara and Kathy examine what is involved in setting up special events for clients. They come up with a list of skills that an events "expert" should excel in, and Sara promises that she will help Kathy get more experience through some of her regular work assignments. She also suggests that Kathy look into taking some seminars on television production and videotaping that will help her gain knowledge in these areas. She tells Kathy to look for such classes on her own and promises to be on the lookout for her also. If the classes qualify, Sara tells Kathy that she will request that the company pay for them.

Sara is careful to make sure that the plans they make will not detract from Kathy's performance in her present job. The more they speak, however, the more the two women become enthusiastic about the goal they are setting for Kathy. Sara has always been appreciative of Kathy's talents. She realizes that if Kathy can concentrate her talents in this area, eventually the department can expand its client services in special events, and the results will mean more business for the company. This has turned out to be a very productive meeting.

Now, let's see how Sara can help Kathy even if Kathy is unsure of what she wants to do next with her career.

Sara: Let's talk about where you see yourself headed over the next few years, Kathy. You started two years ago as a public relations assistant and now you've moved up to an associate position. You've done very well in reaching the goals that you set for yourself a year ago. What's next? Can we make some plans for the future?

Kathy: Gee, I've been thinking about it, but I'm really not sure where I go from here.

Sara: Well, let's think. As an associate you've moved from supporting senior staff members to working directly with clients. As I've said, your performance has been excellent and you show a lot of potential. What aspects of the job most interest you?

Kathy: Well . . . I really liked helping Scott with the anniversary celebration for the Fine Arts Museum. And the work I did on the telethon was very rewarding, too.

Sara: Now we're getting somewhere. What was it you liked about those two assignments?

Kathy: Well, I was involved in a variety of activities, and I liked seeing them all come together in the end into one event. I liked the excitement involved, and I feel I work well under that type of pressure.

Sara: I agree with you. Scott was impressed with the help you gave him, and so was I.

Kathy: I guess if I could pick my assignments, I'd always choose to work on some sort of special event for a client. Hey, do you think that would be possible?

Sara: What do you mean, exactly?

Kathy: Being a type of Special Events Coordinator. You do feel I have talent in this area, right?

Sara: Yes, I do. But that position doesn't exist at the moment. Tell you what, let's explore the possibilities involved in preparing yourself for your dream job. I'll bet there is a lot of overlap in what you'll be working on in your present job, anyway.

By picking Kathy's brain a bit and asking her to think about what she likes in her job, Sara is able to bring out what Kathy's ideal career goal would be.

WORK OUT A PLAN

Once you've identified an employee's "dream job" or future career objective, you can work out a plan of action that will include gaining experience, obtaining training, and whatever else is needed. Take the employee through it on a step-by-step basis. (For an example of a Job Objectives Worksheet, see Figure 4-1.)

1. Examine the list of objectives that was identified at the previous interview. Evaluate the progress the employee has made in reaching these objectives.

2. Determine which objectives need further work. Discuss what obstacles have prevented the employee from reaching any objectives. Decide if time frames set for reaching objectives need to be adjusted.

3. Discuss objectives that have been reached. How has that improved the employee's skills and performance? What are the next levels the employee will now aspire to reach?

4. Discuss whether the employee's ultimate career objective remains the same or has changed. How will this affect the objectives that have already been set?

5. Set new objectives for the upcoming year. Discuss what the employee needs to learn to reach these objectives and how the employee can obtain the knowledge and experience needed.

6. Assign responsibility for reaching these goals. Let the employee know to what extent you will help him or her and what the employee must do independently.

7. Pick out a starting point. One of the most common reasons that "new objective lists" are not acted upon is that in the end the employee is left with such a large task that he or she ends up doing nothing about moving ahead with the goals. Therefore, if you can decide together on a first step that will start the employee toward reaching a tangible goal, you have a much better chance of seeing the employee achieve success.

8. Make plans to meet again. Agree to meet with the employee in one to two months to evaluate his or her progress.

COUNSELING THE PLATEAUED EMPLOYEE

Eventually, some employees reach a point at which they have risen as far as they are likely to go within their organization. Whether they lack the ability, skills, or education to achieve more, or whether they have simply found the position that

Figure 4-1.   Kathy: Job Objectives Worksheet.

Ultimate Goal: To become Special Events Coordinator

Interim Goals	Plan of Action	Progress Made
1. To become more knowledgeable about videotape and film production.	Take courses given at local college. Be available for in-house assignments.	
2. To gain experience in all aspects of special events coordination. This includes preparing displays, organizing meetings, creating publicity opportunities, expanding contacts.	Continue on-job training. Take on assignments involving these types of tasks. Be more outgoing and aware of making contacts in different fields that can be used when setting up special events.	
3. To learn more about other auxiliary businesses involved in special events such as catering, photography.	Get involved when these types of businesses are contacted during special events. Concentrate on observing different suppliers and evaluating strengths and weaknesses of these businesses.	

Proficiency is the key . . .

4. To interest more clients in investing in setting up more special events to promote their businesses, products, and clients.

Formulate plans and work up presentations involving special events for specific clients.

suits them best, counseling these employees during appraisal interviews can require different tactics from the supervisor to keep these employees motivated and interested in their work.

In order to reach what we call a *plateau*, an employee must attain a high degree of proficiency in his or her position. Chances are that there is little need to improve the employee's job skills and that the employee has a great deal of experience in all aspects of the job. If the employee does not wish to move ahead, and, indeed, is truly best positioned where he is, are performance appraisals then a waste of time?

Obviously, we have to answer that with a no. For this type of employee, the performance appraisal becomes more of a semiannual renewal of commitment and statement of purpose than a session in which you work on planning goals for the next step up the ladder. But that doesn't mean that the appraisal cannot be valuable.

The employee who knows he is staying in his current position is probably especially in need of positive reinforcement. Because the work may no longer be very challenging, the employee may have forgotten how essential it is and also may not realize that you appreciate being able to depend on him for consistent and high-quality work.

and positive reinforcement is important.

And just because the employee is not looking to change positions does not mean that he can never take on any new roles in the department. Are there any new responsibilities the department is taking on in which this employee can become involved? This would be a perfect time to discuss such possibilities.

One role that this type of employee traditionally enjoys is that of trainer or mentor to a newer employee. If individuals are paired well, this type of arrangement can add new dimensions to the employee's job that will increase his morale and job satisfaction. It can certainly be rewarding to teach and train another employee—as long as the older employee receives recognition for his efforts.

Employees who have been with their departments for a long time usually have a very good understanding of how things are run. They can be ideal for delegating some of the more routine supervisory tasks, thereby freeing up some of your own time for more pressing matters.

The important thing to remember during an appraisal for this type of employee is to stress the positive and let the employee know how much you count on him or her. Don't be afraid to ask if the employee has any ideas on how the job can be made more challenging, or if there are any responsibilities that are outside his or her current position that are of interest. You may be surprised that if you can get a good discussion going, there is still some room for change on the employee's agenda.

CHAPTER 5

DOCUMENT, DOCUMENT, DOCUMENT

**"Documen-
tation" is
the buzz
word.**

Have you ever sat down to work on an evaluation of one of your employees for an upcoming performance appraisal and have your mind go blank? Of course, you know the employee well. You know what he has been working on for the past four weeks and . . . what else? What did go on with that employee in the past six months or a year?

Well, you should *never* experience this type of anxiety again. Because it is mandatory to giving productive performance appraisals that you keep an up-to-date journal on each of your employees. The buzz word here is "documentation."

You probably have a number of reasons why you may agree with documentation of employee performance in theory, but in practice you just don't need it. Let's look at some of the reasons often cited and tackle them one at a time.

Excuse #1:
I have a very good memory. I won't forget what my employees do; therefore it's a waste of my time.

Fact:
Even people who have a good memory will remember most sharply those events that are most recent. In order to properly evaluate an employee's performance, you need to look at the entire work period, not just the last two months.

Excuse #2:

I have only a few employees. You're referring to supervisors of larger departments than mine.

Fact:

No. We mean all supervisors regardless of how many employees you manage.

Excuse #3:

It takes too long. I have better ways to spend my time.

Fact:

If you schedule a specific time period each week, you can get it all done quickly. A bonus may be that you will do some improved organization of your time. An exception: Document dramatic events immediately; otherwise you may update each employee journal once a week or once every other week.

Excuse #4:

My employees will resent my writing about them. They'll think I'm a spy.

Fact:

The journal is to document every type of performance—good and bad. In fact, supervisors who keep journals tend to evaluate employees more favorably, because they are reminded of good decisions that are easily forgotten or overshadowed by an isolated error.

Excuse #5:

I hate to put things like that in writing. It could come back to haunt me later.

Fact:

The only reason to have this feeling is if you don't know what is appropriate to include in an employee performance journal. That information is covered in this chapter.

START AT THE BEGINNING

Employee journals should include two types of information: incident reports, which document specific events that involve the employee, and progress reports, in which the supervisor comments on and evaluates work in progress. The sample forms in Figures 5-1 and 5-2 can be adapted for your own use.

Ideally, an employee's performance journal is started as soon as he or she is hired. Include in the journal the employee's original job application and resume and some thoughts you had that led you to make the hiring decision. Also include the written job description for which the employee was hired.

If you have never kept a journal to document employee performance, you can create one for each of your employees, regardless of how long they have been with you. Don't be upset if you don't have the job application and resume. It's not vital that you go back to the very beginning. It is helpful, though, if you can, to list all positions the employee has held in the organization and to include a formal job description of each one. Even if the employee has been with the organization for many years, it can give you some interesting insight to read descriptions of each position he or she has held. Likewise, it is interesting for the employee to read those descriptions and see just how far he or she has progressed over the years.

The initial setup of each performance journal may be a little time-consuming, depending on the number of employees you supervise. But once that is done, keeping up with performance documentation need not take very much time.

The most efficient way to document employee performance is to choose a convenient time period and stick to using that time to update the journals. Say, for instance, Friday mornings are relatively quiet. Mark on your calendar that every Friday morning at 10:00 (or alternate Friday mornings) you will close your door and update the journals. Then, clear your desk, arrange to have calls answered, and get to work.

It is not necessary that something extraordinary happen for you to mark it in the journal. Just having a summary for a two-week period such as "Irv worked very independently

Figure 5-1. Sample employee performance journal—incident reports.

Employee Name: _____

Position: _____

Date Hired: _____ Starting Salary: _____

Date	Event	Action Taken	Result	Follow-Up

Having the dates and times down on paper can eliminate a lot of denials and accusations.

the past two weeks and seems to be making progress on his latest assignment" can help you when you are trying to evaluate how well Irv manages his own time for his performance appraisal. Without that note, you may have a feeling that Irv works well alone, but you might not be sure just how you came to that conclusion.

By remaining diligent in your documentation, you will end up with a journal for each employee that truly tells a story about how that employee functions in the workplace. It will be an invaluable tool for your performance appraisals.

IT SERVES AS PROTECTION, TOO

In addition to its usefulness in employee evaluations, your journal can also be used for your own protection and protection for your company if you are accused of bias or improper behavior by an employee or by another manager, and a lawsuit is brought forth. Any incidents that are out of the ordinary or that involve a significant clash of tempers or personalities should be included in the documentation.

In fact, to further protect yourself, you should ask the employee involved in an altercation or unusual incident to read your documentation of the event and sign to indicate that the facts are correct. This will prevent such incidents from being distorted at a later date. It will also keep you from overemphasizing the incident at a performance review if your document is accurate.

For example, suppose you ask an employee to work overtime and he refuses. Just make a note of it in the employee's journal, including the excuse, if any, that was given. (You should also keep track of how many times the employee does agree to work late.) If this happens a number of times, it may become significant enough to make an issue of it. In fact, it is best not to wait for an appraisal if refusal to work late or another type of uncooperative behavior becomes a pattern. By noting it in the journal, you can keep track of

Figure 5-2. Sample employee performance journal—
progress reports.

Date	Current Projects	Evaluation of Work, Problems, Successes, etc.

Make a choice based on performance and experience, not personality.

whether or not the employee is meeting an obligation to work late as it is understood to be a part of the job. If you determine that the employee is not cooperating in this regard, ask him or her to meet with you privately and point out the problem, using the documentation to substantiate your position.

During a future performance appraisal, you will then discuss how the employee reacted to your criticism and whether or not the problem remains or has been eliminated. It is imperative that any significant problem not wait until a formal review to be discussed. Remember, a cardinal rule of productive performance appraisals is *"no negative surprises."*

Another situation that might arise is that an employee may complain that she is not earning as much as other department members because you have not given her overtime assignments. If you have a record of offering overtime and the employee refusing it, the journal has served to protect your position.

IT KEEPS YOU OBJECTIVE

Maintaining documentation of your employees' performances also can come in very handy when you are faced with such difficult decisions as laying off a department member or choosing an employee for promotion. Before making any such decision, it is best to go over the documentation on all employees concerned in the decision. If you have done a good job, the documentation can help you make a choice based on actual performance and experience rather than personality. Take Carol's case, for instance.

Carol supervised a group of six salespeople for a growing toy manufacturer. Although base salaries of the six were the same, the sales staff earned different amounts according to the commissions they received. For that reason, there was competition among them as to who would be given the most desirable territory.

When a new sales territory opened up, Carol was torn over which employee would get it. The region bordered on territories covered by three of her people.

Mark was the most flamboyant of the group. His charming manners and good looks helped a great deal in pitching sales. He knew the market and boasted in the office that he placed the product in 75 percent of the stores he visited.

Erica was quieter, but her sales record was good. She was consistent in bringing in orders, but she was modest. When Mark boasted of a new sale, she just smiled and congratulated him. She never shared news of her own successes.

Jeffrey did well, but at first sight you might be surprised that he sold toys. A rather humorless man, his demeanor never hinted at the possibility that he ever had any fun.

At lunch with another sales manager, Carol discussed the decision she would soon have to make about the new sales territory.

"Between the three, it barely seems to be a contest," said Evan, who knew all the members of Carol's department. "Mark has it all over the other two. He could sell ice to the Alaskans, couldn't he?"

"Actually, it's very interesting that you say that," said Carol. "I used to believe that myself, but about eight months ago I decided to keep a performance journal on each of my salespeople. I found reading them over yesterday pretty insightful."

"What do you need something like that for?" asked Evan. "Don't their sales figures speak for themselves?"

"Not really. You have to take into consideration the territories they work and the different products they are each asked to push. It's not always as easy to judge as picking the highest order placer. Besides, I've included additional information in these journals."

"Like what?"

"Well, like how many days are spent on the road and how

often they are in the office doing papework or whatever. I've also kept track of expense accounts, and I've included feedback I get on each of the employees from clients."

"Really?" Evan was curious. "So what did you find?"

"I found that Mark is not the top salesman he purports to be. He's good, but we have someone who is better."

"That quiet Erica?" guessed Evan.

"No. It's Jeffrey. All things considered, he deserves the new territory the most," said Carol.

"Old Stone Face. Who'd have thought that?"

"Please, Evan, watch what you say."

"Sorry, it's just that from the looks of things, you'd never pick him as the top producer."

"I agree. But when I compared everything about the three, his position on top came out very clear. Now the hard part will be breaking the news."

"Don't worry about it. If you've really got the facts to back up your decision, you're in good shape," said Evan.

"You know, you're right. Those journals really did come in handy after all."

It's not hard to see how Carol could have made a different choice if she had not had the performance journals to rely on. Personality, brag stories, even an employee's looks can have a strong effect when you must make a choice among people. Basing most choices on the facts is a safe and fair way to decide, and accurate, appropriate documentation will be very helpful to you.

For details of what information should be included in a journal and what should not, take the quiz below on the Ins and Outs of Journal Keeping. Not everything you see belongs in an employee performance journal. Certain information is very important, but including some observations could get you in hot water. Do you know the difference?

INS AND OUTS
OF JOURNAL KEEPING

	In	Out
1. Data on employee attendance, lateness, extended lunches.	_____	_____
2. Rumors circulated about employee.	_____	_____
3. Data on what employee works on, including project names, coworkers, outside contacts, and any feedback on employee relevant to job performance.	_____	_____
4. Unsupported complaints by others against employee.	_____	_____
5. Data on overtime worked and/ or offered to employee.	_____	_____
6. Any disciplinary actions or verbal warnings given to employee.	_____	_____
7. Personal comments about employee, including any judgments about fashion, hairstyle, or how "good" or "bad" an employee's appearance may be.	_____	_____
8. Facts about employee's personal lifestyle—whether employee is married or single, a parent or not.	_____	_____
9. Noteworthy successes or failures of employee on the job.	_____	_____
10. Training courses taken and/or offered to employee.	_____	_____
11. Your opinion on what employee should do regarding his or her career.	_____	_____
12. Your impressions of the quality of employee's work. Include facts about work that support your opinions.	_____	_____

13. Your interpretation or analysis   _____   _____
    of "why the employee does
    what he or she does."

14. Details of discussions with the   _____   _____
    employee about any policy
    infractions.

Compare your answers with those that follow.

The bottom line is that when you keep an employee performance journal, stick to the facts. Your personal feelings or opinions about the employee may remain with you, but they should not be written down in the journal. Anything that borders on a personal comment or one that can be construed to show prejudice or bias should be kept out of the journal.

When documenting disruptive or damaging incidents, include as many of the facts as you can. In cases of disciplinary action, write up exactly what transpired, what action was taken, what was discussed. Then have the employee sign the documentation for the record.

Answers: 1. In; 2. Out; 3. In; 4. Out; 5. In; 6. In; 7. Out; 8. Out; 9. In; 10. In; 11. Out; 12. In; 13. Out; 14. In

CHAPTER 6

PREPARE YOURSELF

We won't deny that conducting performance appraisals can indeed set you up to feel quite foolish or ill at ease. It's understandable after all that you are uncomfortable facing someone you work with every day and passing judgment on how well he or she performs that work. Granted, your position gives you the right to do it, but it's human nature to squirm a little.

However, if you've taken the time to prepare carefully for each performance appraisal you hold with your employees, you don't have to feel foolish. Use the two checklists that follow (Don't Start Without It and Do You Know . . . ?) to make sure that you are ready before you start your meeting.

CHECKLIST: DON'T START WITHOUT IT

Use this checklist to make sure that you have everything you need handy before you start your performance appraisal.

____ Employee performance journal
____ Record of employee attendance
____ Employee job description
____ Completed employee evaluation forms
____ List of job and career objectives drawn up during the last performance review
____ Blank paper and pen for taking notes

Some automatic structure eases that first session.

_____ A recent example of employee's work (when appropriate)

_____ Examples of work problems you want to discuss

_____ List of available training courses appropriate for employee

_____ Manual of company policies and rules

CHECKLIST: DO YOU KNOW . . . ?

Go over this checklist to determine whether you know all you need to about your employees before holding an appraisal meeting. Don't wait until the last minute; give yourself time to find the answers you need.

_____ Employee's length of service with company

_____ Current projects employee is working on

_____ Progress employee is making in current project

_____ Employee's educational and experience background

_____ Date of employee's last promotion

_____ How employee relates to coworkers, clients, and others

_____ Level of employee's technical skills

If you've taken our advice and given the employee a self-evaluation form and filled out a complementary one of the employee yourself, you've taken the first step to make the meeting less awkward. Why? Because you've set up some automatic structure for the session.

Going over the job analysis with the employee allows you to discuss the work that the employee does on a daily basis. If the two of you disagree on the relative importance of specific job aspects, it will come out now, and it will also give you the opportunity to discuss any problems the employee is having performing the various job responsibilities.

AVOIDING ERRORS IN PERFORMANCE REVIEWS

If you think back to what you've most disliked about some of the performance appraisals you've been subjected to yourself, you can help make sure to avoid the errors of those who have gone before you. Some common mistakes that supervisors make when giving performance reviews are:

• *A patronizing attitude.* Supervisors who come across as if they know exactly what is best for the employee in terms of career growth and development without asking the employee's personal goals will generally be tuned out. In fact, the employee is apt to feel resentful and take the opposite of any advice given.

• *Stressing the negative.* Some supervisors believe that it is their responsibility to point out everything the employee is doing wrong. The performance review is the appropriate time to discuss real problems, but it is also imperative that you talk about what the employee is doing right. And think about your complaints before you speak. Are they really significant? Remember that anything negative you say during a performance appraisal will have a lasting effect. Make sure it's worth it.

• *Lack of information.* Supervisors who don't know what their employees are working on or what problems they are having are actually caught off guard at performance appraisals.

• *Comparing employees.* Leave other employees out of the discussion it at all possible. Talking about how good other employees are compared to the one being reviewed is asking for trouble. It is not a productive technique.

• *Concentrating on the money.* Performance appraisals should not center on salary. This is the time to evaluate performance and plan future objectives.

• *"Winging it."* Unless you have a plan for what you want to say to the employee, the performance review will come off exactly as it is, an off-the-cuff discussion of the employee's performance. Know what are the most important issues you want to discuss with your employee. Make an outline or a list of points you want to cover and refer to it during the session to make sure you don't leave out anything important.

• *Giving misinformation.* Not wanting to appear less than perfect, supervisors too often make the mistake of providing answers to questions whether they know the answer or not. Remember, you'll be seeing the employee tomorrow, and you can get the answer for him or her then.

• *Being inconsistent.* Again, unless you take the time to plan what you want to stress with the employee and what the final result of the meeting will be, you run the risk of giving inconsistent evaluations and messages. This is not to say that a performance review is either all positive or all negative, but it requires forethought to make it a valuable message.

BE PREPARED

The better prepared you are for the performance appraisal, the more productive your discussion will be. The Job Analysis and Performance/Work Habits Review forms (Figures 3-1 and 3-2 in Chapter 3) will help you to gather your thoughts on the employee's performance and focus in on what areas you want to emphasize. Likewise, if you have been diligent about documenting the employee's performance, the time to reread this journal is before the meeting. Just having it handy during the meeting is fairly useless unless its contents are fresh in your mind. You don't want to have to start searching through the journal to find documentation on a particular

Remember: Both you and your employee are adults.

event, so read it and mark the pages that you want to show the employee.

In addition to getting current on the employee's performance and job responsibilities, you also need to anticipate questions or concerns the employee will have about work and about career opportunities within the company. If you have set career objectives with the employee in the past, you should have a written record of them. Locate this list and discern whether the employee has made any strides toward achieving these objectives in the past six months or year. If you have changed your mind about the likelihood of the employee being able to reach these goals, formulate in advance what you want to say to the employee on the subject.

KEEP AN ADULT LEVEL

One of the most common reasons supervisors come off appearing awkward or uncomfortable during performance reviews is that they feel obliged to take a paternalistic or maternalistic stance when speaking to the employee. This does not have to be the case.

Remember that your employees are adults and, therefore, they have as much right to have their opinions and feelings taken as seriously as you have. Consider why you are in the position of supervisor. Chances are it is because you have the most experience and knowledge about your particular field. However, this does not extend to all or any areas outside the workplace. Just because you know the most about phototypesetting or sales or scientific research does not mean that you know the most about life or even that you can make all the rules regarding behavior.

You may feel that because you are the supervisor, your employees should automatically follow your career advice. That is not so. If you come off being dictatorial and telling your employee what he or she should do, you are probably only accomplishing the building of resentment. But if you

At the center of the discussion is the employee's livelihood. It's not a time for jokes or idle chat.

hold a discussion in which you and the employee can exchange ideas on an adult-to-adult level, the results may be very rewarding.

Your employees can benefit from your experience, but they will undoubtedly resist doing so unless it is their own choice to make. Therefore, instead of presenting the employee with a set agenda to follow, ask questions, elicit opinions and feelings, and invite the employee to pick your brain so that together you can make some career decisions for that employee.

The language you use is another factor that affects how you are perceived by your employees. Resorting to cliches or "parental-sounding" phrases will sometimes alienate people and cause them to believe that you are just spouting jargon instead of relating directly to them as individuals.

Like it or not, the performance appraisal is a time when it is important to get serious. Even if you have a very easygoing relationship with your employees, this should not spill over into the appraisal interview. At the center of the discussion is the employee's career and livelihood. It's not a time for jokes or idle chat—even if that's what makes both of you more comfortable.

Many employees will spend very little time on their own thinking about what they ultimately want out of their careers. Neither do they consider how they can improve what they are doing in their present jobs to further those careers or just to improve productivity and therefore feel justified in requesting more money. It is up to you to insist that the employee take the time during (actually beginning before) the meeting to concentrate on himself now and really think about how he can plan to improve and grow on the job.

Most of us do feel uncomfortable being serious. It's certainly easier to be funny and make light of things. But take heart, it's not against the rules to smile, be friendly, and make a joke when appropriate. Just make sure that the true purpose of your meeting is accomplished.

CHAPTER 7

PREPARE YOUR EMPLOYEE

A prepared employee will give you a better session.

Until now, your employees have probably experienced performance appraisals as something that happened *to* them, something that was *given to* them. Well, no longer. A productive performance appraisal requires the cooperation and collaboration of both the supervisor and the employee. But you can't expect your employees to be able to jump right in and give themselves an objective evaluation. You're got to prepare them to be able to participate in the process.

In Chapter 3, we introduced the Job Analysis form (Figure 3-1), which should be filled out by you and also given to each employee. Check back to Figure 3-1 to recall what types of things are to be entered on the form.

The purpose of the Job Analysis form is for both the employee and the supervisor to come to an agreement on the major job responsibilities of the position held, and also the relative importance of each job function. When you find there is a large difference of opinion here, you often have significant problems between the employee and the supervisor. Going over this form gives you a chance to straighten out these problems.

Give the employee the form in Figure 3-1 and ask him to list his major job responsibilities and areas of accountability, the purpose of this activity, and the "weight" or amount of time spent and relative importance of this responsibility within his particular position. Tell him that you will be filling out the same form and that you will then compare what you both have written when the two of you meet three or four days later.

The Performance/Work Habits Review (Figure 3-2) should also be completed by both you and the employee. Ask him to give as honest a self-evaluation as possible. Remind the employee that it may be hard to assess one's own abilities and that the purpose of this form is just so that you can both get a sense of what areas need work and what skills are the best developed.

SET THINGS STRAIGHT

Just giving the employee the forms in Figures 3-1 and 3-2 and setting a convenient date for an appraisal interview are not enough to prepare your employee. Consider how the following supervisors handled the same situation. Which one of them do you think did a better job?

[Vicki]

Vicki: Hannah, your semiannual performance appraisal is coming up and we're starting a new method for doing this. I'd like you to take some time to think about your job and how you would rate your own performance. Fill out these two forms and bring them with you when we meet for the appraisal. I've set aside next Tuesday afternoon at 2:00 P.M. Is that okay with you?

Hannah: Yes.

Vicki: Fine. Let me know if you have any questions before then.

[Drew]

Drew: Rachel, as you know from the memo I sent out last month, we're going to be handling performance appraisals differently from the way we've done them in the past. I want your input on how you feel you've been doing and also on what you want to be doing in the future. I'm going to ask you to fill out these two forms and bring them with you to our appraisal meeting. Are you free next Tuesday at 2:00?

Rachel: Yes.

Drew: Great. Now, the purpose of the first form is to allow us to come to a consensus on exactly what your job responsibilities are and how you feel about their different priorities and importance. The second form asks you to rate yourself on various job skills and work habits. I know it's hard to judge yourself, but remember, this is not a test and this is not the last word on anything.

These forms are meant strictly to identify strong and weak points. I will not be basing any salary increases on what you write here. Also, I guarantee that there will be areas where we disagree. The important thing is that we work together here to come up with a personal improvement program and new job objectives so that you can keep growing and learning.

Rachel: Okay. I understand, Drew.

Drew: Great. Now, I want you to look these forms over and come to me with any questions before you start. Remember, this is still a new process for me, too. We're going to learn it together, okay?

Rachel: Okay. Thanks.

It's really quite obvious which supervisor did the better job in preparing the employee to begin the process of productive performance appraisals. One thing Drew mentioned is an excellent idea for introducing the whole concept of productive performance appraisals to your employees, that is, a memo.

Once you have decided to commit yourself to trying a more productive, collaborative method of conducting performance appraisals, it is very helpful to distribute a memo for your staff members that prepares them for the changes that will be coming soon. For an example of such a memo, see Figure 7-1.

Figure 7-1. Memo: introducing new performance appraisal procedures.

Memo: To All Department Members

From: Supervisor

Re: Performance Appraisals

Beginning next month, we will be initiating a new system of performance appraisals in order to make these semiannual meetings more valuable for everyone involved. Before meeting with me for your appraisal, you will receive some self-evaluation forms, which I will ask you to complete and bring to our meeting.

We will also be discussing your job and career objectives, and I ask that you please come to your appraisal meeting prepared to speak on these subjects.

If you have any questions about these forms, please ask me for help right away. I believe that we can make performance appraisals more productive and meaningful, but I will need your cooperation. Thank you.

SETTING GOALS

In addition to asking the employee to fill out the job analysis and self-evaluation forms (Figures 3-1 and 3-2), also make sure that your employee knows that you intend to speak about her personal career objectives and that the two of you will work on devising a new action plan together. If you have done this in the past, you might want to provide the employee with a written list of the goals that you both had set during the last review and ask the employee to think about what progress had been made toward those goals, what goals she would like to change, or where, if any, she would adjust the priorities that have been set.

Many people feel resentful about being asked to set new objectives for their job performance.

Unfortunately, many people feel resentful about being asked to set new objectives for their job performance. "What's wrong with the job I'm doing now?" they ask. "Why do I have to change?"

The honest answer here is that people *do* need to change, that growth on the job keeps it interesting and helps both the employee and the department to work more efficiently. What you have to get across is that you are not asking your employees to set new objectives in order to punish or reprimand them for not performing well. The reason for setting new objectives is so that employees will continue to feel a sense of achievement and satisfaction in the work they do, so that employees can continue to work toward higher salaried positions, and so that employees can increase their value to the company and in the outside job market.

PART III

COMMON PROBLEMS AND EFFECTIVE SOLUTIONS

CHAPTER 8

WHEN YOU DISAGREE ON ROLES AND GOALS

Recognize that you may each have a separate agenda.

More often than it would seem likely, employees and supervisors have entirely different perceptions of the employee's job responsibilities. The longer these misunderstandings go on, the greater will be the ultimate damage to the employee's morale and to the well-being of the department. The Job Analysis form (Figure 3-1 in Chapter 3) has been designed to pinpoint and eliminate these very problems. But first, let's look at some of the reasons why this type of disparity exists in the workplace.

TITLES—A MATTER OF SEMANTICS

What happens when an employee is hired or promoted? He or she is given a title, correct? But with that title often come beliefs and definitions that vary according to the person using it. Consider some of the many "title" words that abound in the workplace: assistant, associate, manager, administrator, senior, junior, trainee, vice president, analyst, partner, junior partner, director, researcher, assistant manager . . . and these are just the very general terms. Within each profession and business there exist more delineations that may more closely define the person's functions, yet still leave many details to the imagination.

If you are bound to follow whatever came before you, when do you make the time for improvement?

PRECEDENCE—IS IT SET IN STONE?

Another determining factor in what is considered to be part of someone's job is invariably what that person's predecessor accomplished. If Rose, as associate bookkeeper, was always responsible for payroll and taxes, does this mean that every subsequent associate bookkeeper is responsible for these tasks? That may depend on how you choose to handle it.

Following precedence is an easy trap to fall into. It follows that time-honored adage, "If it's not broke, don't fix it." But sometimes the simplest way is not the best. The sharp supervisor will realize that each new employee hired and each promotion that is made open up the opportunity to revise and refine the inner workings of the department. If you are bound to follow whatever came before you, when do you make the time for improvement?

Precedence can also play an unfair part when you are guiding employees in setting career goals. Do you find yourself automatically showing an employee how to take the same steps up the job ladder that her predecessor did? If you are committed to having a productive meeting, you must disregard such temptation and collaborate with each employee on an individual basis without preconceived ideas. Even if the end results have been the same for the last three employees who held that position, it is your job to give that fourth, fifth, or sixth employee the benefit of the doubt and plan for his future based on his individual needs, desires, and abilities.

DISAGREEMENTS ON THE JOB DESCRIPTION

It is precisely because employees and supervisors often disagree on the exact roles of the employee that we suggest that these roles be established at the onset of the performance appraisal. Without coming to a mutual understanding of what the employee is responsible for and the relative importance of each task and skill, it is impossible to hold a cohesive discussion.

Be sure to have the employee's job description on hand when discussing a disagreement you have over that employee's responsibilities. The job description can often solve minor problems that tend to be misunderstandings over what is expected of the employee. However, in a productive performance appraisal, you should be prepared to reevaluate the employee's job at each appraisal and be open to amending the written description to more accurately reflect the employee's position.

When you review the Job Analysis form (Figure 3-1) with your employee, you will find that there are two types of discrepancies. Either you and the employee have a significant difference of opinion in the fundamental purpose of the position, or you disagree about specific tasks and whether they are actually an integral part of the employee's job. Let's first examine the more serious situation—disagreeing about the fundamental role of the employee in the department.

Suppose your employee has the title of assistant researcher. Your understanding of the position is that her major job function is to support and assist the staff's senior researchers. However, it is clear from the employee's performance, and also from the Job Analysis form, that the employee believes the most important part of her job is the independent, smaller research projects she is also given to work on. What should you focus on in this situation?

First, recognize why there is the difference of opinion between you and your employee. In this instance, you may each have a separate agenda. You, as the supervisor, view an assistant researcher as skilled support staff whose job it is to make the work of the more senior staff members easier and more productive. The employee, however, if she is ambitious, sees the position as a temporary one that will lead to a more senior position in due course. Therefore, the employee is more interested in completing independent assignments in which she can prove her ability to succeed.

Certainly, both of your opinions are understandable. But it is up to you to blend the two of them into an agreeable arrangement. Use what the employee has written in the Job Analysis form to clarify what she believes is the more important function of her job. Then state what you need from her in terms of support services and the reasons why she is needed there. Is the employee concerned that you will not be open to promoting her after she has proven herself ready? Discuss the circumstances and assure her that she can be judged by the support she gives senior members as well as by the independent projects she does.

AGREEMENTS ON THE JOB DESCRIPTION

If your employee is very insistent about wanting to work on independent projects, it is best to be open to this suggestion and make arrangements for the employee to be given the opportunity. You do, however, have the right to explain that he may have to wait some time for promotion and that it cannot be an automatic event that occurs after a predetermined amount of time.

Disagreeing about the responsibility for specific tasks can also cause a temporary obstacle in conducting your appraisal. Too often, employees feel resentment at being asked to do things they believe are not part of their job. Once these feelings are brought out into the open you can settle these matters and repair any damage that may have been done.

Before getting on the defensive, take the time to determine if an employee's resentment toward any specific task is justified. Why is the employee complaining? Do coworkers at the same level have the same responsibility, or is this employee singled out? Is there a question of an employee being asked to perform a specific task based on gender? This can be a particularly sensitive issue and such assignments should be avoided. Does the employee feel he is being held back professionally because of required tasks that may not

Employees have opinions, too.

reflect the progress he has made? All of these possibilities need to be considered before taking a stand.

If you've decided that regardless of the employee's feelings, the task in question is legitimately part of his job, take a stand firmly but dispassionately. It is when personalities get involved and the supervisor is tempted to throw his or her power around that such situations make permanent rifts in the employee-supervisor relationship. Explain your position matter-of-factly and request that the employee cooperate in continuing to be responsible for the task. It is important that you not make a big issue out of "winning" here. Go on to the next topic as quickly as you can—preferably to something in which you are in agreement.

CLASHING ON GOALS

Chapter 3 presented an example of an employee and a supervisor in agreement over performance goals to set for the employee. But what happens when that is not the case? What do you do when an employee has ideas about goals that you believe are very unrealistic, or does not agree that improvement is necessary?

Before you answer this question, keep in mind that no matter how certain you may be about something, the employee also has a right to his or her opinion. You should try to guide your employees, and you can set standards of performance that must be met. However, unless you can convince the employee to "buy into" your plan, performance will suffer.

Let's look at one example of how to handle this situation. Barbara is in an assistant's position in a financial planning firm that caters to middle-income clients. She is mainly involved in researching investments and analyzing portfolios to help senior staff members prepare recommendations for their clients.

Al: Barbara, tell me, have you given much thought to how you think you can improve your job performance? I'd like to work on setting some goals for you so that we can make sure you're getting the experience and training you need for the future as well as for the job you're doing now.

Barbara: I feel that I'm very competent at my job. The only problem I see is that I don't get enough of an opportunity to take on greater responsibility. I'd like to work with clients more than I've been doing.

Al: Really? I'm surprised to hear that. I believe you're still not fully comfortable dealing directly with clients. I believe you need to be surer of your abilities and more fluent in the marketplace before you take charge of a project.

Wisely, Al is cautious about sounding too critical of her ideas. He wants to hear more of Barbara's thoughts before forming an opinion.

Barbara: Oh, I've been doing a lot of work on my own to prepare myself to work with clients. Actually, I've been reading a lot of business magazines lately, and it seems that if you want to make money, you've got to be the one who handles it. I'm ready to show our clients how to handle it.

Al: That's an interesting theory. I don't recall you took many finance courses in school. Am I right?

Barbara: That's true. But real-world experience counts for something, doesn't it? I've learned so much since I started working here.

Al: Yes. But I feel you still have a lot to learn. Our business is too risky to learn as you go, since it involves other people's money. You need to continue researching investments and analyzing client portfolios under close supervision before you take on that responsibility.

Barbara: Well, sure, but when do I get to make some decisions? How will we know when I *am* ready?

Al: That's a good question. I think what you're really telling me is that you're a little impatient to move ahead with your career. I can appreciate that. I'm going to ask you to continue learning through experience for three more months. At that time, if you and I feel you are ready, I will assign you to work with a senior staff member on a client portfolio in which you will be able to make suggestions. Then, you, I, and the senior staffer will go over your choices together to evaluate if they are in the client's best interests.

Barbara: But I want to get involved in working directly with the clients. Can I start on that, at least?

Al: You certainly have a lot of ambition. Slow down. Client contact is a very delicate matter. It's quite easy to scare off a client by being too aggressive or just saying the wrong thing. Let's arrange for you to begin sitting in on counseling sessions a few times a week, okay? Afterward, I'd like to discuss with you what you've learned from the meetings. I want to make sure you're completely ready before I let you solo.

Barbara: Well, I guess that makes sense. But I still feel that I'm more ready than you think.

Al: I appreciate your frustration, but you're going to have to go along with me on this. If I let you do something that I didn't believe you are capable of, I wouldn't be doing either of us any favors. Now, do I have your commitment that you will continue to work on these skills over the next three months?

By keeping his cool and hearing what Barbara was *really* saying, Al was able to avoid putting her on the defensive by coming out and criticizing her plan. Although he has doubts about her present abilities, he is willing to be more aggressive in training her to take on more responsibility, since she obviously has the desire. However, Al is careful to maintain control over the situation. He makes it clear that she will not be given any more autonomy until he is absolutely convinced that he is being fair to a client by placing the client in

Barbara's hands. Barbara may not ascend her career ladder as quickly as she would like, but Al is going to make sure that she's ready for whatever she takes on.

Helping employees choose goals that are most appropriate for them is basically a matter of listening and asking the right questions. You can use this list of do's and don'ts as a guide.

- DO: Ask employees to fully explain their career plans and the reasons behind their formation before offering an opinion.
- DO: Repeat an employee's goals that you may not agree with so that the employee can hear what it sounds like aloud (this can actually make a difference).
- DO: Help an employee to choose goals that you will be comfortable helping him or her to achieve. When personal goals clash with what is best for the department, offer alternatives that can satisfy both parties.
- DON'T: Only offer your own plan toward success to the employee. Collaborate together, letting most of the ideas be formulated by the employee. The employee will be more committed to a plan that he has devised himself.
- DON'T: Be afraid to give your opinion when asked. Be aware, though, of any prejudices you may have and remember that even though something may not be right for you, it could be right for the employee.
- DON'T: Be judgmental if an employee chooses to take a path different from your own. Be objective and consider only whether the goals are in the best interest of the employee and the department.

ASKING THE RIGHT QUESTIONS

The best way to get someone to change his mind to your way of thinking is to get him to come to that conclusion on his own. When employees choose inappropriate goals, or if they have trouble planning for the future, you can help them by asking the right questions to get their minds going in the right direction. See Questions About Goals listed below, which you may be able to use in your own discussions with your employees. There is space for you to add questions of your own—particularly questions that deal implicitly with your organization or line of business.

Questions About Goals

1. What would you like your next job title to be? How do you think you can best work toward reaching that goal?
2. Are you interested in taking any courses on the outside? Would you be interested in attending training seminars available through the company?
3. What long-range goals would you set for yourself? How are you working toward reaching those goals now? What do you plan for the future?
4. How is your present job preparing you for the goals you are setting? Is your present job setting the right foundation or is there another path that you might consider that might be easier to pursue?
5. What do you know about the requirements for the goals you have set for yourself? Do you need to find out more?
6. Where do you think you would ultimately find yourself if you did not actively seek to change your career course? What would be the pros and cons of such circumstances?
7. What career changes will you have to make to reach the goals you are setting? Can they be made within the boundaries of your present position?

8. _____

_____

_____

9. _____

_____

_____

10. _____

_____

_____

CHAPTER 9

WHEN THE NEWS IS BAD

Pamela: We both know that there have been problems with your performance. Although we've discussed what's wrong on several occasions, let's use this time to see if we can clarify where your performance needs improvement and make plans to bring you up to a satisfactory rating.

William: But I *have* been trying. Do you mean that I can't get a satisfactory rating this time?

Pamela: Yes. I wish I could tell you otherwise, but I believe that this does not come as a surprise to you.

William: Well, not really.

Pamela: William, I'd like to give you another chance. Let's not dwell on the past except to identify the problems and see how we can correct them. From today on, we have a fresh goal to reach. Starting today, you are going to improve your work performance. In six months, I want to be able to share good news with you when we meet for your performance review. How does that sound?

William: That sounds fair.

Pamela: Fine. Now, have you filled out the forms I've given you? Let's see where we are in agreement and where we are not.

You would probably agree that giving a performance appraisal to a poor performer is one of the more unpleasant tasks of being a supervisor, but like it or not, it's part of the job. The good news is that a productive appraisal can be an effective tool for turning around that employee's behavior.

In the case above, Pamela confronts William head-on with

It may be hard for employees to admit they're not performing well.

the news that he already knows—that his general rating of performance is unsatisfactory. But rather than spend time berating William for the past, Pamela suggests that they use the appraisal to correct William's problem performance. She also makes sure to give William a strong warning that his performance must improve if he wants to remain with the company.

Fortunately, Pamela has been doing her job all along. Instead of waiting until his review, Pamela and William have already discussed the problems with his performance, and she has tried to make him aware that unless he improves there will be consequences to pay. But like many people, William seems to need the lesson of a poor performance rating before he takes the situation as seriously as he should have.

Although William may have chosen to ignore his unsatisfactory performance until now, at this point he seems ready to admit the problem and work toward changing the situation. This is primarily because he was expecting to hear what Pamela had to say.

From this point on, Pamela can follow the same pattern she would with any other performance appraisal, discussing how to improve performance, setting productivity goals, and planning for the future. Many times, however, employees will deny that they are not performing up to the standards set for the department. If you are not prepared, you can spend a lot of time just arguing the point of whether or not the employee is truly underperforming. When you are faced with this type of employee, turn to the following guidelines to keep the meeting productive.

A QUESTION OF ATTITUDE

Sometimes we think an employee is a poor performer, but when we sit down and try to rate his performance, we find that his skills and abilities are more than adequate. Instead, we realize that the problem the employee has is a question of attitude.

Have prepared a list of changes you would like the employee to make.

GUIDELINES FOR AN APPRAISAL WITH A POOR PERFORMER

• *Have documentation available.* Mark entries in the employee journal with paper clips so that you can quickly show examples of problems the employee has had with performance and/or behavior over the past six months.

• *Make sure you have also documented the times you have spoken to the employee about his or her performance.* This should put an end to any insisting by the employee that he or she was unaware that any problem existed.

• *Have written quality standards to show to the employee.* (These standards should be distributed to all employees at hiring or when a promotion is given.)

• *Show the employee examples of how his or her work does not meet the standards as well as the work of others.* This will protect you against any accusation by the employee of unfair or prejudicial treatment.

• *Have prepared a list of changes you would like the employee to make in his or her performance.* Don't just say "You have to improve." Be specific on exactly what needs to change.

• *Be positive about the employee's ability to improve.* If appropriate, arrange for extra training or closer supervision by yourself or a senior co-worker. Present this idea to the employee not as a punishment, but as a solution to the problem.

• *Set new short-term goals for the employee.* You may also want to identify some long-term goals to give the discussion a positive feeling, but tell the employee that for the present time he or she should concentrate on these short-term goals and that when improvement is made you will meet again to plan on how to obtain future goals.

• *Be honest with your employee about his or her future without being patronizing or admonishing.* Spell out exactly what the employee has to do to improve and what the consequences will be if he or she cannot change the performance. If an employee's job is in jeopardy, say so, not as a threat but as a warning that he or she must be given. Not only is this fair to the employee, but it is essential to protecting yourself and your company in any legal actions a discharged employee may file in the future.

• *Make a "contract" with the employee to improve performance within a certain amount of time.* Set measurable standards for the improvement and plan together exactly how this can be accomplished. Agree to meet again in two months to assess the progress that has been made.

Some attitude problems do actual damage to performance. For example, if an employee has a surly attitude that is displayed when he interacts with customers, this certainly can adversely affect business. In contrast, arriving late to an office, being inconsiderate of others, or being careless with company property may not directly affect the employee's work, but they are probably disruptive to the rest of the department and can definitely damage the morale of the employee's coworkers.

Discussing an attitude problem with an employee is probably a more uncomfortable situation than citing inadequate performance. It puts you in this awkward position of a parent reprimanding a child when you should be able to deal with each of your employees on an adult level.

You can get past this dilemma by refusing to treat the employee like a child and stating the problem without voicing any judgments about it. The following guidelines can help you plan what to say.

DO'S AND DON'TS IN DISCUSSING ATTITUDE PROBLEMS

Don't Say	Do Say
Your personality is too abrasive to your coworkers and to me.	You need to speak more respectfully to both your coworkers and your supervisors.
I don't like your attitude.	Your behavior shows that you seem to resent doing the work that is asked of you. If that is not true, you need to change your behavior. (Cite specific examples.)
It's too bad you'll never succeed with your attitude.	You have the ability to do well and succeed. You need to change the behaviors that are standing in the way of your success.

It is best if you can avoid the word "attitude" altogether, as it has such a patronizing tone. The truth is, you and the employee will both know that it is his or her attitude you are discussing, but if you keep the emphasis on specific behaviors *you have documented,* you eliminate the opportunity for him to say that you are "picking on him" or that you are "misinterpreting his actions."

DEALING WITH EMOTIONAL OUTBURSTS

Occasionally, an employee will have such unrealistic expectations or perception of her role that she will react very strongly if disappointed with the review that is given. This can unnerve even the most experienced manager. Crying, shouting, walking away, or clamming up are all reactions that can be very difficult to deal with. Here are some suggestions for getting through such a situation.

• *Crying*. An employee in tears is probably not able to discuss things calmly. Try to minimize the employee's embarrassment by not becoming agitated. Offer compassion and a box of tissues, as the problem of crying is usually compounded by the need for tissues. Ask the employee if she would like to talk a little later, or give the employee time to recompose herself by leaving the room for a while.

• *Shouting*. Don't answer shouting with more shouting. Instead, talk calmly, slowly, and firmly to the employee and do not appear frightened. If the shouting continues on without abatement, ask the employee to leave and say that you will continue the discussion when he has had time to calm down. If you feel threatened physically, by all means call security for assistance. You are not obligated to get hurt under any circumstances. Don't feel as if you have to be a hero if someone is truly out of control.

• *Walking away*. Although it is impossible to have a discussion if your employee walks away, it may not be an entirely bad thing. Some people know they cannot face an issue and they leave rather than completely lose their temper. Don't try to physically restrain someone who walks out on you. You can ask the person to please stay so that you can finish the discussion, but if he doesn't care to listen, don't force the issue. Let the employee leave and take up the discussion again when he has calmed down.

• *Clamming up*. An employee who is feeling a lot of hostility or resentment toward you may react by avoiding talking to you altogether. Here, again, you need to be the more mature person. Talk to the employee about whatever you need to, but don't push the issue by attempting to make small talk. It is best not to make too big a deal out of this, because chances are it will pass before too long. If, however, the situation continues, you will have to address the em-

Follow-up is essential, especially with a poor performer.

ployee directly and request that she talk to you so that you can put the problem behind you.

THE IMPORTANCE OF FOLLOW-UP

Although follow-up is important with all employees, it is even more crucial when dealing with a poor performer. Such employees have been dealt a blow to their egos—to their self-confidence—and they need continual guidance and reassurance that they can succeed on the job.

Once you have identified the problem and charted a course for the employee to follow, don't look to constantly find fault with the employee's work—you made your point at the performance appraisal. If you are satisfied that the employee's attitude is good and his motivation is real, try to point out what he is doing right and encourage him to keep it up. You needn't keep reminding the employee of his past failures. If you have counseled the employee well, it is now time to accentuate the positive.

The problem most supervisors have with giving poor performance reviews is that they feel it is their job to, in effect, scold the employee for his or her actions. Instead, you need to take the attitude that you are going to work with the employee to plan how to improve performance without being judgmental over "why" there exists such a need for change. Treat the employee like the adult he or she is, and if the employee is truly willing to work hard, you are likely to be happy with the results.

CHAPTER 10

WATCH OUT FOR PITFALLS

Sexual harassment has become such a sensitive issue that supervisors need to be extra careful.

"A beautiful woman like you can go very far in this company if you make the right connections."

Who said that? Was it you? We hope not. No matter how innocent or even flattering you may mean a remark to be, commenting on an employee's appearance is absolutely forbidden during a performance appraisal (and is almost always out of line at other times, too). Sexual harassment has become such a sensitive issue in today's workplace that supervisors need to be extra careful not to say anything that can be interpreted as suggestive or threatening. It may be second nature or well meaning for you to comment on a woman's new hairstyle or clothing, but it has no place in a performance review. If it is your practice to begin the meeting on a complimentary note, compliment the work your employee has done recently. Beginning an appraisal meeting by saying "You're looking great today" is not acceptable office etiquette.

And this is not exclusively a man/woman issue. Women are also being accused of harassing men, and anyone can be subject to accusations of homosexual harassment.

Does the above make you afraid to open your mouth? It really shouldn't. It is just very important that you think before you speak and that you keep all discussion during performance appraisals on a professional level.

Sexual innuendo is just one of the pitfalls that can trap a supervisor if he or she is not careful. Let's go over some of the more common and most dangerous ones so that you can avoid making any serious mistakes.

KEEP IT STRICTLY BUSINESS

We've already pointed out the dangers of making any remarks that can be construed as sexually or romantically suggestive, but other types of personal remarks can also get you into trouble.

Religion and politics have traditionally been sensitive subjects of conversation in a social setting. If you bring these topics up in the office, you are playing with fire. Don't ask your employee what he thinks of the upcoming election as an icebreaker during your performance appraisal meeting, and refrain from asking any questions about the employee's religious holidays—especially if they differ from your own.

Even seemingly neutral topics such as real estate or vacationing do not belong in the appraisal interview. The reason that these topics are objectionable is that if you ask certain types of questions, it can be interpreted as actually seeking information about the employee's finances—something that is not your business. You can inquire about the well-being of an employee's family, but don't get into a discussion on family planning or size lest you be accused of being prejudiced against an employee who seeks to expand his or her family and further "burden" the company with medical insurance premiums and maternity leave.

Another hazardous area to watch out for is when the discussion begins to include other people in the office. Although you may think the employee will keep whatever you say in confidence (after all, he said he would never repeat anything you discuss), don't take the chance. Office politics is too tempting a subject for gossip, and anything the manager says about anyone else is really too good to keep to yourself.

If an employee tries to get you to explain why you did this or that for a coworker, why he or she deserved that promotion over himself, don't fall into the trap. Bring the subject back to the employee himself and speak about why you've taken the actions (or lack of actions) on the part of the employee based on his performance, experience, knowledge, etc. Even though one employee will view him- or herself as the equivalent of another employee, that does not mean that you must justify your decisions based on this premise. Say something like "Let's talk about you, not her" and bring the discussion back to where you want it to be.

During a performance appraisal there is such a thing as being too honest. Don't use this time to make any negative comments about an employee's appearance, style of dress, or personal habits unless it has a direct bearing on performance (as, for example, if an employee is required to wear a uniform and it is not cared for properly). Although you may feel you are doing the individual a favor by suggesting that she pay closer attention to fashion, it can come back to haunt you if the employee decides you have discriminated against her on those grounds. Stick to the issue of performance during the appraisal. If you must make personal observations, do it within another context.

Small talk aside, you can get into real trouble if you're not careful what you say even when you do stick to business. The biggest pitfall you can fall prey to is to make a promise to an employee that you are unable to keep. No matter how casually you may think your promise was made, we guarantee that your employee will take it as seriously as an oath written in blood. Therefore, be sure to think twice, and then once again, when promising an employee any of the following:

- Money
- Promotion
- Training programs
- Improved assignments
- An upgrade or change of office or work space
- New equipment

This is not to suggest that you cannot commit yourself to producing anything but only to warn you that you must be sure of your ability to make good on any promise that you make. You can promise to *try* to do something for your

Keep money out of the appraisal process.

employee during a performance appraisal, but make it very clear that you do not know if you can succeed and that the employee should not count on anything until you are able to find out for certain.

Many times, employees will ask questions that you cannot answer during an appraisal. If things have been going very well, you may not want to put the employee off and you may be tempted to guess at the answer. Don't do it. Remember what was discussed earlier. Anything you say, no matter how noncommittally, will be interpreted as a solemn oath by your employee. At best, you will have to return to the employee and retract your statement later. At worst, you can do serious damage to your relationship with that employee—and possibly with all the others with whom the employee shares the incident.

DON'T TALK DOLLARS

Although the most pressing detail every employee will want to know is "How much of a raise can I get?" we advise that you keep money out of the appraisal process until the follow-up meeting, discussed in Chapter 11.

A productive performance appraisal must focus entirely on the employee's performance—the identification of strengths and weaknesses, and the development of new goals and objectives for the near and far terms. Once money comes into the discussion, interest in talking about how the employee can improve will quickly dissipate.

When the employee does bring up the subject of money, state that you will discuss it at a later time and that now you want to concentrate on performance only. If the employee insists, you can further explain that you do not make the final decision about money and that you will make your recommendation based in large part on the outcome of this current meeting.

Let the employee know that, like it or not, you can exert a

much greater influence in how the employee achieves his or her personal career goals than in the exact salary the employee receives. With some exceptions, salary increases generally have to meet certain company guidelines, and there is not a great deal of flexibility to work with.

Watching out for pitfalls requires more than just making sure you don't bring up the wrong subject. You are just as likely to say the wrong thing in response to a question or a statement made by an employee. To see if you recognize a pitfall in time, answer the examples in this exercise in the next section.

THE TROUBLE ZONES

It can happen to the most careful manager. You may know exactly what to say and what not to say, and yet an employee may bring up a subject that can get you into a lot of trouble if you give the wrong answer. Below are some examples of questions you may be asked. We've answered the first two and left the rest for you. How good are you at avoiding the trouble zones?

EXERCISE: AVOIDING TROUBLE ZONES

Question:
"Why did Adeline get promoted last month when I've been here two months longer than her and I'm still waiting?"

Sample answer:
"It was not a choice between the two of you. Let's stick to talking about you. I'm sorry, but I don't think you're ready for promotion just yet, and I'll explain why."

Question:
"Gee that's a nice new suit, you look like you've been working out or something."

Sample answer:
"Thank you. Now, getting back to business . . ."

Question:
"I'm really interested in that new training program for secretaries, but I heard you have to get recommendations from three managers. Could you get me into the program?"

Your answer:

_____

_____

_____

_____

Question:
"My last supervisor promised me a big raise at my next review. Now that I've been transferred to your department, will that still be true?"

Your answer:

_____

_____

_____

_____

Question:
"I used to enjoy working with Andy, but lately he's been difficult to deal with. I think he's been drinking again. What do you think?"

Your answer:

_____

_____

_____

_____

Question:

"I really need to get a promotion soon. You know what it's like, being a single parent yourself. There's just never enough to go around."

Your answer:

_____

_____

_____

_____

Question:

"What are you going to do about filling Tina's spot if she doesn't come back after her maternity leave? Aren't I next in line?"

Your answer:

_____

_____

_____

_____

PART IV

WRAPPING IT UP

CHAPTER 11

THE POSTAPPRAISAL MEETING

You've made it through the session; you've dodged the pitfalls and managed to honestly communicate with your employee. Together, the two of you have established some new short-term objectives and have refined the long-term career goals to suit new interests and new perceptions of opportunity. You're ready to close the books on this performance appraisal, aren't you?

Sorry, not so fast. You must still hold a final meeting to discuss salary and upcoming plans for new assignments, training, changed behavior, improved performance, and anything else that surfaced during the interview. It is in this meeting that the employee receives a final rating. Let's go back to see how Harvey and Matthew did from Chapter 3.

Harvey: I believe we've covered quite a lot today, Matthew. Although I was mainly pleased with your performance before, I think we've worked through the few trouble spots we have. Your overall rating for this review period is a 4. You can see on this form how I arrived at that grade. If we can act on what we've discussed, I think things will really begin to pick up for you.

Matthew: What about my raise? Can you tell me how much that will be?

Harvey: Not yet. I have to finish my review paperwork and discuss the details with Henry, who takes it to the personnel department. The raise is based on the employee evaluation and also the plans for the employee's work over the next six months to a year.

Matthew: I see. Well, I'm really anxious to find out. When will you know the amount?

Harvey: Let's meet again Thursday morning at 10:00. Can you make it through three days?

Matthew: I suppose so.

Harvey: Great. At that time, we'll go over the salary and also firm up some of the plans for the future that we made today. In the meantime, I'd like you to go over the list of goals we set today and think about if there is anything else you'd like to do that would help you meet these goals—something perhaps we didn't think of today. I'll get right on the paperwork I have to do and have the answer to your questions on Thursday.

Matthew: Okay. Thanks, Harvey. This was an interesting meeting.

Harvey: Thank you for your cooperation. You've made it an interesting process for me, as well.

Harvey does a good job in ending the performance appraisal interview. Notice how he uses "we" instead of "you" when he talks to Matthew about improving performance and reaching new goals. By doing so he shares in the responsibility of making these improvements—something responsible managers should be doing.

Harvey has done a good amount of work since his meeting with Matthew. First, he has completed the overall review form, which he will submit to his own boss and to personnel (see Figure 11-1 for a sample form). He also has determined exactly what he will do in order to help Matthew improve his performance and reach the new goals he has set.

In addition, he has written up a final draft of the performance and job objectives he and Matthew agreed upon during their meeting and included a copy in the documentation of their meeting. A copy will also be given to Matthew.

Finally, Harvey will meet with his own manager to discuss Matthew's compensation. The more thorough a job Harvey

Figure 11-1. Sample employee appraisal form.

Employee: _____

Position: _____

Rating Key: Excellent—5, Very Good—4, Satisfactory—3,
Needs Some Improvement—2,
Unsatisfactory—1

Job Responsibilities and Areas of Accountability Identified and Performance of Each Rated

Job Responsibility	Functional Objectives	Rating
1 _____		
2 _____		
3 _____		
4 _____		
5 _____		
6 _____		
7 _____		
8 _____		

General Work Habits and Attitude: Enter a rating of 1–5

Attendance/punctuality   _____
Meets deadlines   _____
Cooperates with coworkers   _____
Accepts supervision   _____
Manages work schedule   _____
Uses equipment properly   _____
Prioritizes work well   _____
Job performance   _____
Quality of work   _____

Ability to solve problems   _____
Uses original ideas   _____
Communication abilities   _____
Time management   _____
Technical/professional knowledge   _____
Hands-on skills   _____
Interpersonal skills   _____
Ability to work on a team   _____

• Goals achieved since previous appraisal:

_____

_____

_____

• New areas of responsibility employee has been given
  or will soon be given:

_____

_____

_____

• Performance goals and/or problems identified:

_____

_____

_____

• Career goals identified and revisions made, if any:

_____

_____

_____

• Plans and recommendations made for additional training or experiences:

_____

_____

- Manager's overall rating of employee's job performance

  (1—5): _____

  Explanation: _____

  _____

- Manager's recommendation for future:

  _____

  _____

  _____

- Salary increase recommended: _____

I have read this review and understand what is written:

Employee's signature: _____

Manager's signature: _____

Date: _____

does on the first three steps, the better equipped he will be in making a case for a generous increase for Matthew. However, had the opposite been true and Matthew had received a poor performance review, Harvey would need to do just as thorough a job to explain why he was recommending a minimum or zero increase at this time.

DISCUSS GOALS FIRST

It will be tempting, especially if you have good news for the employee, to start off the postappraisal meeting by announcing the salary increase that has been approved for the em-

**Your em-
ployee is
entitled to
see the
final rating
he has been
given.**

ployee. However, if you can get the employee to hold out just a little longer, you can use the time to finalize plans you have made and to obtain the employee's strong commitment to reaching the goals that you have set together.

Your employee is entitled to see the final rating he has been given. Have the employee read over the review form and ask any questions he or she may have. At this point, you should make it clear to the employee that you have taken the employee's opinions and concerns into consideration and that you will not be making any changes in the evaluation form. Although we have stressed the collaborative aspect of a productive performance appraisal, this does not allow you to abdicate making a judgment on the final rating of the employee's performance. Reading this appraisal form is strictly for informational purposes so that the employee can understand how the rating, compensation, and promotion systems operate.

Next, present the employee with the list of objectives and career goals. It is also helpful to give her the list that was made a year or six months ago so that the employee can see if and how it has changed. Now is the time to go over these goals again and clarify anything that you may need to. State again how you plan to help the employee reach these goals and express your wish that she will remain committed to reaching them as well. Encourage the employee to voice any concerns that she has about the new objectives, asking if she has contemplated what you discussed at your last meeting.

If your future plans for the employee include a new type of training, try to have as much information as possible about the program he will be entering. If you can give an exact date, or at the least, the month it will be in, you will have given the employee something very concrete to anticipate.

If you and the employee have set precise goals for promotion, it is wise to once again go over exactly what requirements must be met before a promotion can be granted. If promotions cannot be given unless a specific opening exists, this must be made very clear to the employee.

THE STATUS QUO

Money is often a distraction!

As often as not, the end result of a performance review will be that an employee's job will not have any substantial changes and that you are actually encouraging him to maintain the status quo. This presents a special challenge during the postappraisal interview, as you may not have any entirely new goals to cheer the employee on to accomplishing.

When this is the case, take this meeting as another opportunity to express your appreciation for the dependable, consistent good work that the employee has been doing. Reiterate goals for the employee to gain more experience and knowledge and to continue to be a valuable member of the department.

With all employees, utilize the postappraisal interview to again emphasize your interest in the employee's personal and career growth by offering your assistance with these goals. Thank the employee for her cooperation in making the performance appraisal a productive work session and express your confidence that she will be able to act on the plans that have been made.

SAVE THE MONEY FOR LAST

The reason that we strongly suggest you save informing the employee about his or her salary increase for the end of the discussion is simple: Once you share the decision, the employee is likely to be very distracted. It's human nature. Once you give an employee a dollar amount, he or she will undoubtedly be doing complicated mental calculations, trying to determine if now he or she can buy that car that's at the top of the list.

And you will know immediately whether the employee had been expecting more or less than the amount you have promised.

If you have done your job well up until this point, the amount of money involved should not come as a great surprise at either extreme of the spectrum. If your employee had been expecting a lot more, ask yourself if you either said anything to give him false expectations or if you failed to make sure he understood the level of satisfaction you have with his performance.

Although the postappraisal interview is the time to finalize plans and intentions that were brought out during the review, don't feel that it must be the end of the process until six months or a year have passed. The reason that many performance problems continue is that managers neglect the daily reactions and feedback employees need in order to change their behaviors. Check in with the employee regularly to see if progress is being made. If you're not pleased with the results, talk to the employee seriously about what else can be done. Keep the review process going on a steady basis.

CHAPTER 12

YOU'RE READY TO GO

We've now taken the productive performance appraisal from beginning to end. As you can see, our recommendations do not include any shortcuts in handing out appraisals. On the contrary, we espouse a system that may very well be more complicated and involve more work than you have done in the past. But we strongly believe that you will find the results are worth the effort.

If your job as a supervisor or manager were just to make sure the work got done, you might be able to argue against making the effort to collaborate with your employees in evaluating their job performances and setting goals for the future. But your job should involve more than that. Recognizing that *employees*—not machines, technology, hardware, or money—are your organization's most valuable resources means that you need to work with them to help them do the best work they possibly can. For that, they need your input and guidance. You can give it to them by following the advice mapped out in this book.

Now, let's review the steps you need to follow to successfully conduct productive performance appraisals.

1. *Set goals and identify responsibilities from the onset.* At the time an employee is hired, or when a promotion or transfer is given, sit down with the employee and *write down* all the job responsibilities the employee will have. You can also identify areas of weakness and set goals for giving employees training and experience that will allow them to grow in these areas.

2. *Document employee behavior and performance.* Keep a current journal on each of your employees (no matter how small your department may be). Include positive and negative incidents and note any disciplinary actions or warnings that are made to the employee.

3. *Prepare employees to participate in the review process.* Provide your employees with self-evaluation forms well in advance of the appraisal interview. Remind them of what will be discussed during the meeting and ask that they give thought ahead of time to future goals and to questions regarding current job concerns.

4. *Prepare yourself for the review process.* Don't set the interview for a time that you will be rushed or subject to multiple interruptions. Have ready all necessary and pertinent documentation. Read documents before the meeting. Consider future plans for the employee and write them down so that you can present them to the employee at the meeting. Try to anticipate what concerns the employee will want to discuss. Clear desk and office of distractions. Don't try to "wing it." Set an agenda.

5. *Have an open mind about your employee's future goals.* Allow the employee to make a case for an idea that may not be on your list and try to help the employee plan how to reach these goals. You may also suggest your own ideas. Remember, this is supposed to be a collaborative process.

6. *Do not discuss compensation until the postappraisal meeting.* At this point, make sure you have firm commitments from management or personnel to any salary increases, training programs, promotions, or transfers that you wish to give the employee. Make no promises that you cannot absolutely deliver.

7. *Follow through the plans you make with the employee with daily supervision and feedback.* Make the appraisal process a continual one, particularly when you have positive comments to make. Check progress employee is making toward reaching goals and hold follow-up sessions to rethink strategies if employee progress is not satisfactory.

We've given you a blueprint for making your employee appraisals productive ones. The execution is up to you.

WHEN WILL I FIND THE TIME?

Does all of this seem overwhelming? It might. We've written down just about everything you need to do to make your employees' performance appraisals valuable and productive. However, now that you've read through the book, you can ask yourself just how much of what we've discussed is already part of your management techniques.

Chances are, you're already doing a lot of what we've suggested—at least in part.

For example, you may be documenting only disciplinary problems. It won't be very hard to expand your documentation to include performance. Or, you may already be involved in setting job and career goals for your employees. We've now given you a way to incorporate this directly into the review process.

We've given you a blueprint for making your employee appraisals productive ones. The execution is up to you. Think about what you want for your employees. Consider the difference it can make in your department to have employees who are truly committed to improving their job performance and who believe that their manager is committed to helping them to do so.

RATING YOURSELF

Are you confident that you now know the difference between a productive performance appraisal and one that does little more than provide a superficial review? In the following exercise are statements a supervisor might make during an appraisal.

EXERCISE: WHAT'S THE DIFFERENCE?

If you believe the statement is a productive one, mark it yes; if not, mark it no. Check your answers with the key below.

	Yes	No

1. "I think your best bet is to follow the path that Susan took. She started out just like you and look how well she's doing now."

2. "What do you see as your biggest strength on the job? How do you think you can build on that?"

3. "There's no room now for any promotions. You're going to have to find satisfaction in your present job."

4. "You're doing everything just fine. I really have no complaints at all. Any problems on your end?"

5. "Your performance has been very good. I'm especially pleased with the way you interact with clients. For example, when Mr. Jones was upset last week, you were able to calm him down and minimize any damage to the business relationship."

6. "You've really shown tremendous ability in understanding the new technology. Have you given any thoughts to getting more involved in that end of the business?"

7. "I can't agree with your assessment that you are diligent about meeting deadlines. I can show you several incidents in this journal when you did not get your work done on time and I had to give you an extension."

8. "That's just not a realistic goal. No ____ ____ one I know has ever done it like that before."

9. "I can't help but take your poor per- ____ ____ formance personally. Haven't I given you every chance to do better?"

10. "I believe you can do better in meeting ____ ____ quality standards. Why do you think you're having so much trouble in this area?"

Answers

1. No. What another individual chose to do can be entirely irrelevant. It is better to give a reason that relates to the employee.

2. Yes. This engages the employee in thinking about him- or herself and in participating in the evaluation process.

3. No. Approaching the subject in this way accentuates the negative. No one likes to be told what they "have" to do.

4. No. This statement pretty much closes off the discussion.

5. Yes. Follow praise with an example of what the employee is doing right. It teaches the employee to keep up the good work and also lets him know that you are aware of what he's doing.

6. Yes. Again, this is being aware of the employee's talents. It also opens the discussion and thought of a new avenue of opportunity for the employee.

7. Yes. Disagreement is followed up with evidence from the employee journal. That's the way to do it.

8. No. Goal setting should be a collaborative effort. The employee should be free to explore

new goals even if the manager does not immediately view it the same way.

9. No. Never take an employee's poor performance personally. This statement sounds more like a parent trying to shame a child than a manager speaking to an employee.

10. Yes. Criticism is stated by positively saying the employee can do better. The employee is given a chance to explain herself before the manager makes further criticisms.

**Do you
need to
fine-tune?**

A FINAL CHECKLIST

What steps can you take to improve your present appraisal system? Does it need a complete overhaul or will it hold up with some simple adjustments? We've given you the beginning of a checklist on how to improve your system. You fill in whatever else is necessary.

_____ Create a system for documenting each of my employee's job performance.

_____ Provide employees with forms to evaluate their own work.

_____ Improve communication with employees so that "performance appraisal" are not dirty words.

_____ Become more familiar with training programs that can help my employees grow in their occupations.

_____ Improve my listening and processing skills so that I can better collaborate with my employees on making plans for performance improvement and goal setting.

_____ Practice being more aware of pitfalls in open discussions with my employees. Think before I speak.

_____ _____

_____

_____

_____ _____

_____

_____